# Ethical Leadership for Better Education System

What kind of people run our schools? What makes them behave as they do? What kind of an example do they set? How can headteachers live up to expectations? What makes them fail? What keeps the profession in good standing in the taxpayer's eye, and what undermines it? *Ethical Leadership for a Better Education System: What Kind of People Are We?* sets out a new vision for school leadership, moving beyond 'leadership styles' and 'best practice', to the motivations of school leaders. It proposes a way for the profession to embrace, develop and maintain ethical standards.

Chapters:

- Explore the 2017–18 Ethical Leadership Commission, considering the core values and virtues, principles and behaviour we should expect from our school leaders

- Provide a clear, ethical code for thinking about reinforcing ethical standards among school leaders

- Look at the tensions between professionalism, accountability and *in loco parentis*

- Discuss structural change in the education system over 20 years

- Open discussion and reflections on the dilemmas facing ethical leaders and how to tackle them

- Demonstrate a way through the accountability pressures headteachers face, drawing on personal experience

- Place practical issues within the context of the whole system

Considering the future vision of educational leadership, *Ethical Leadership for a Better Education System* will appeal to all levels of school leaders, existing and aspiring. It should help everyone who leads in school, and everyone who cares about the models we set before the nation's young.

**Carolyn Roberts** is headteacher of Thomas Tallis School, UK, her third headship. She led the Ethical Leadership Commission in 2017–18.

# Ethical Leadership for a Better Education System

## What Kind of People Are We?

Carolyn Roberts

Routledge
Taylor & Francis Group

LONDON AND NEW YORK

First published 2019
by Routledge
2 Park Square, Milton Park, Abingdon, Oxon OX14 4RN

and by Routledge
52 Vanderbilt Avenue, New York, NY 10017

*Routledge is an imprint of the Taylor & Francis Group, an informa business*

*British Library Cataloguing-in-Publication Data*
A catalogue record for this book is available from the British Library

*Library of Congress Cataloging-in-Publication Data*
A catalog record for this book has been requested

ISBN: 978-1-138-50441-7 (hbk)
ISBN: 978-1-138-50442-4 (pbk)
ISBN: 978-1-315-14600-3 (ebk)

Typeset in Melior
by Apex CoVantage, LLC

Printed and bound in Great Britain by
TJ International Ltd, Padstow, Cornwall

# Contents

# Acknowledgements

This book could never have happened without so many teachers and headteachers who have taught me. I particularly name Gordon Dunstan and Stewart Sutherland, professors at King's College London who taught me ethics and philosophy. My lasting thanks also to Mike Grimitt and John Hull of Birmingham University School of Education.

I have taught in Birmingham, Coalville, Peterlee, Pimlico, Houghton-Le-Spring, Durham, Hartlepool and now Greenwich. School leaders have been optimistic enough to take me on; children, teachers, staff and governors have worked patiently with me.

I'm particularly grateful to the heads who mentored me into becoming a head, Richard Bloodworth and John Dunford, and the tireless deputy heads who've put up with me working out how to do it.

The Association of School and College Leaders and the Ethical Leadership Commissioners committed themselves to the foregrounding of ethics in education at a time when the profession most needed it.

To my children Mark and Miranda who support me so kindly despite my irascibility and inability to think straight on Thursday nights. And my fascinating, opinionated and learned husband Jonathan, without whom this book would never have reached publishable state. He's read and commented on it several times but like everyone else above, bears no responsibility for the opinions herein.

This book is dedicated to my mother and grandmother *Audrey Parkin and May Davidson*, teachers both.

# At the school gate

Stand outside any school in the morning and you see what schools are for. Children and young people in various stages of wakefulness pour through the school gates, dressed in whatever garb they, their parents or the school reckon suitable for learning. There's often a cheery type hallooing 'Good Morning' usually by name, and there may be another less cheery soul checking the sort of stuff that school has decided to check on the gate. For younger children, crossing the bar from one side to another may be accompanied by a kiss, a fond smile, a worried look. For adolescents the sleepy frowning trudge stands in for the happy skip.

One day you might see a parent storm past the adults at the gate and into reception. Perhaps she's dragging a child by the hand, perhaps he's shadowed by a surly adolescent with her arms folded. The question is always a version of: 'An outrage has been perpetrated. What's the school going to do about it?' Reception staff triage the demand and perhaps the head is produced, or an available representative: class teacher, head of year, assistant or deputy. The problem's talked through and, with luck and good systems, resolved. If not, parent and child might depart with as much gusto as propelled them thither to seek a better reception at the County Hall or MP's surgery, much luck may it do them. Or Ofsted or the local paper, while angrily tweeting and posting.

Who is involved in this and what do the players represent? The parent is the taxpaying citizen. He has expectations of what the school should provide. The class teacher or head of year is the person to whom the parent hands over the care of the loved little one, no matter how large or small. As levels of seniority increase, staff represent the endeavour of the state in the field of education and child development, with the headteacher as the locally commissioned expert provider of this particular bit of the state's activity, the person in charge of the community's values, trusted to do what's right.

What the school decides to do or not do about the parent's complaint will depend on its beliefs about parents, about behaviour, the incident and the mindset behind its systems. Are there effective procedures and policies, properly implemented, to secure the school's purpose in this community of individuals? And if it is to be resolved, how? On what principles are decisions made?

Most problems stem from human interaction: a classroom procedure is sensible, but a teacher has been dismissive, or incompetent. Or the child is motivated currently by an interpersonal agenda with other adolescents. Or has been brought up to believe teachers to be vindictive functionaries. Or faulty attachment means that the lines between school and home are painful and blurred. Or the parent is angry, miserable, adrift, desperate for a better life for the beloved young.

The school gate is the meeting place of the school and the parent, the state and the child. The school may say it is driven by learning and care but the parent needs to see that in the individual relationship of institution to child. The state wants a quality citizenry: the parent a quality childhood. Both may be driven by the need to improve on what has gone before: better education to give her a good start for adult life, better chances.

The school is the gateway to everyone's best hopes, so there's a lot resting on this argument. You'd better hope the nice lady on reception has a friendly face.

In this book I play fast and loose with titular sensibilities. *Head* or *headteacher* refers to the most senior educational post-holder in a school or Trust, the executive decision-maker, the principal, executive head or CEO.

When I say *we* I mean an abstract or actual collective of those postholders.

*Leaders* are all of the above, including the voluntary non-executive governors and trustees who share the senior professionals' responsibilities.

*Children* are people up to the age of 18, though I sometimes use 'young people'.

# Introduction

Like Ginger Rogers observing that she did everything Fred Astaire did, but backwards and in high heels, headteachers do everything other professionals do, but watchfully scrutinised by children and adolescents. The nation trusts us to form young people into the best that they can be. The public expects us to know what kind of example we should set them. We have a day job with huge implicit and terrifyingly explicit accountability measures. You'd think that to survive we would have to have a pretty clear shared understanding of how to conduct ourselves in the job, but do we? How might we go about making it clearer? Why is it so important?

This book is about ethical leadership of schools, how it is essential, why it is confused and what we might do about it. It's about how school leaders behave. It's about why they do what they do and whether they are prepared, enabled and supported to be the best hope for the child as they take them by the hand through childhood and adolescence. It's about the way they fulfil the public trust placed in them, and the way they model the good life to the young.

Most of all, it's about how they think so that what they do represents humanity at its best. Schools are where society looks after its young until they are old enough to take on the mantle of adult citizenship. This book is about those people who choose to take that responsibility, and how they decide what is right and wrong, good and bad and how they live it in their working lives.

## A brief summary of this book's contents

I hope that you have a few hours to sit and read the whole book from cover to cover. It's also possible that you read the book on the bus, or while deterring loafers behind the gym or waiting for the concert to start after school. I've written it in pieces short enough to stimulate your thought and action, all of which add up to the big argument of the book. I have even included some reflections which may annoy, but I hope encourage you that you are not alone, and may even make you smile.

Here's how it works so that you can make sense of the fragments in the whole.

There are four Parts to the book:

■ **Part 1 Professional school leaders.** I look at the kind of job it is and who it is for, about professionalism, about our work for children, as the state's parents and for society. If we are clear about *what* we're doing and *why*, then it's easier to make decisions about *how*.

■ **Part 2 Ethics and schools.** I discuss how ethics are essential to our work as communities, organisations, places of learning and public bodies. I begin to demonstrate ethical analysis from philosophy, public life and education to define and address some dilemmas.

■ **Part 3 Why is it difficult?** Here I look at the grit in the oyster: why is good behaviour compromised? What kind of people are we, and what have we become?

■ **Part 4 The Framework for Ethical Educational Leadership 2018.** I explore the Framework in detail, and discuss some ethical puzzles. What would you do?

## What are the chapters about?

### Chapter 2: The Framework for Ethical Educational Leadership 2018

This book is was written at the same time that I was Chair of the *Ethical Leadership Commission 2017–18.* It uses its Framework for Ethical Educational Leadership. Chapter 2 sets it out briefly, but it is explored in Part 4 and Chapter 13 onwards, most of the second half of the book.

### Chapter 3: The headteacher as professional

I open **Part 1: Professional school leaders** discussing the absence of any common discourse about heads as professionals. I compare our work with other professionals who work in the best interests of their patient or client. I begin an analysis of our professional behaviour using four dynamics: consent, constraint, expertise, and benefit. I explore three beneficiaries of our profession in Chapters 4, 5 and 6.

### Chapter 4: The professional for the child

The treatment of children (under 18s) is regulated and discussed nationally and internationally. I set our work in these frameworks and particularly in the context of achieving the best interests of the child. Education and learning are at the heart of this, but so is our position as the most immediate and committed public body in every child's life.

## Chapter 5: The professional for parents

I explore the dilemmas of which adult is responsible for the child and what it means when we talk about being *in loco parentis* – 'in the place of the parent'. Are we paradigm parents?

## Chapter 6: The professional for the state

Public money, land, buildings and legislation make duty to the state huge in our lives. Do we provide safe places? How well do we enable learning? And while we are talking about ethics, what do we do for the moral development of the child?

## Chapter 7: Ethical thinking

This opens **Part 2: Ethics and schools**, and specifically discusses ethics, the thinking-through of right and wrong. How might we use the philosophical traditions to make decisions? I review how we use the ethical traditions of rights, duties, virtues and case discussions.

## Chapter 8: Ethics in public life

In this chapter I set out and apply the 'Nolan Principles' maintained and developed by the Committee for Standards in Public Life.

## Chapter 9: Setting English standards in education

What part does ethics play in the *Teachers' Standards* (2012) and the *National Standards of Excellence for Headteachers* (2015)?

You would be about halfway through at this point. I have set up the shape of our work, its social context and the intellectual equipment and legislation which might help. Just before I set out what the Framework expects and how it might work we have a brief reminder of some of the reasons why we need better guidance and practice: **Part 3: Why is it difficult**?

## Chapter 10: Perverse accountability

Quite often heads have said that they do what they do because they must, and that they must because of accountability. That accountability is essential is beyond doubt in a democratic society, but exactly what must we do? I go on to dissect aspects of school performance and examination outcomes: is there a confusion of beneficiaries?

## Chapter 11: What should we do? Using ethics to make better decisions

It's striking when you begin to apply some specific ethical themes to the dilemmas we face. In this chapter I illustrate the point by selecting values and virtues to analyse common leadership decisions.

## Chapter 12: The theatre of education

This is a short recap of the state of the drama before we use the Framework.

## Chapter 13: A Framework for Ethical Educational Leadership 2018

This chapter opens **Part 4: The Framework for Ethical Educational Leadership 2018**. It explains the Framework's origins and development with a brief explanation of the organisations involved and its initial work. I explain how the Framework makes a difference to professional development.

## Chapter 14: Using the Framework for Ethical Educational Leadership

The Framework is a useful toolkit for heads. This chapter shows how each critical tool might be used in practice. In this chapter I begin with an ethical priority and make a connection with real life. My cases bring together a value or virtue and a real issue in pairs:

- Selflessness and pay
- Honesty and examinations
- Openness and governance
- Staffing and objectivity
- Integrity and behaviour
- Accountability and budget
- Leadership and admissions
- Trust and community
- Wisdom and curriculum
- Kindness and inclusion
- Justice and selection
- Service and accountability pressures
- Courage and results
- Optimism and new starts

## Chapter 15: Leadership in the leadership group

I look at the particular issues raised by the practice of leadership. This time I use real life as the starting point with anonymised cases from recent years. I make some suggestions for each one, and then there are some at the end for you to consider with no model answer.

## Chapter 16: Governors and trustees

This chapter reminds governors that ethics in school leadership applies to you. It also specifically discusses Trust and governing boards, and the Headteacher Standards.

## Chapter 17: Creating an ethical climate: learning and reflection.

Here are some ideas about how you might develop ethical reflection in your school. I suggest nine sessions exploring ethics generally and focusing on school management and the character of the school community.

## Chapter 18: Ethics and qualifications

I outline the implications of how we might develop our ethical reflection in learning programmes. The chapter comments on programmes for early career teachers, aspirant leaders (NPQML, NPQSL), and Senior Leaders (NPQH, NPQEL).

## Chapter 19: Who decides?

Being a professional headteacher is quite exposed: the Royal College structure common to medics is just starting to develop for teachers but the ethical framework sets out important elements of the work. I review part of our journey to regulate ourselves like other learned professions.

## Chapter 20: Finally

Your story and my story in education are not the same, but I hope we share common cause and this will help you do good in your work.

## Why you should read this book

Throughout the book you'll find scenarios, case studies, definitions and conundrums. Where there are problems, there are usually many answers. Some of them help children and some of them do not. Most of them, like our daily work, require clear and rational thinking. I hope this book helps you do that, whether your day has begun calmly or crossly at the gate, the threshold of hope.

Any book about ethics in school leadership is hazardous. I'm not sure I get it right so who am I to write for others? Colleagues might think it impertinent and the taxpayer might feel a bit spooked. Don't we know what we're doing? *Wait a minute, don't they know what they're doing? With our children? Schools have been around for centuries but they're just thinking about ethical behaviour now?*

School leadership is a perfect example of the postmodern conundrum so I need to spend a moment on the context in which I write, of deregulation, fragmentation and what is optimistically called the school-led self-improving system.

This laudable statement is packed with assumptions. It reflects a changing landscape since the first state-funded independent 'academy' schools opened at the turn of the 21st century and the largely unified post-war system of Local Authorities was busted open. The speed of transformation may have exposed a vacuum in our shared understanding of what we're doing, why and how we do it. I think expressing that clearly might help us develop a better school system.

In former days, when all schools were run by local government, or the dioceses of the Roman Catholic or established church, the taxpayer could imagine that there was a moral guardian for schools who oversaw the decision-making of school leaders so that it was in the best interest of the child and the state. That might have been the Director of Education, or the bishop. They were assumed to know what was right and wrong, headteachers shared that understanding and when things went wrong the system would sort it out. Whether or not this was true is less relevant than the fact that it doesn't exist any more.

Deregulating a system takes time and shared groundrules. In the years since deregulation blossomed, the taxpayer has been entertained, regaled and outraged by press reports of poor behaviour by school leaders: inflated salaries, nepotism, off-rolling, gaming the examination system, for example.

As this postmodern system settles down, matures, embeds or deteriorates further (depending on your point of view), it might be useful to highlight some of the societal and democratic potholes in the new landscape. A London School of Economics Education Research Group report (West and Wolfe 2018) identify nine. Well might the angry parent at an academy reception desk struggle to know where to take his truculence.

1   Different schools and types of schools have different governance depending on when they were set up 'with no consideration of their present needs'.

2   Academies and Free Schools were designed to bring 'autonomy and freedom' to schools. However, schools now in Multi-Academy Trusts have 'no freedom'.

3   Governors used to be appointed openly and run maintained schools according to public principles of openness. The appointment and processes of 'trustees' are different.

4   Local Authorities with their democratic underpinning and open scrutiny have been replaced by the Department for Education-appointed Regional Schools Commissioners.

5   The 'free school presumption' means that Local Authorities cannot meet children's needs for school places, but are reliant on RSC decisions to fulfil their statutory responsibilities.

6   The 'public notice' system of changing schools' scope or intake is not required by academies or free schools.

7   'There is a lack of reliable information of the way in which the academies policy is working'.

8   Academies do not need to follow the National Curriculum or teachers' pay and conditions agreement. This is 'potentially reducing educational opportunities for pupils' and has 'potential impacts on teacher recruitment in maintained schools'.

9   Academy trusts' accounts are externally audited but do not provide detail; 'this again is a transparency issue and opens the door to possible abuse of funds'.

In such a 'complex and fragmented system' (Barton 2018) therefore, the quality of school-level decision-making is crucial to the quality and probity of the system.

Why? Because such fragmentation means that every school or Trust leader is her own moral arbiter. That might be a good thing in a liberal democracy where people make their own choices about right and wrong, supported by a sophisticated, civilised government and a legal system with checks and balances. But human beings are – well, human – and school leadership is exceptionally pressured because we are dealing with the nation's beloved little ones. Leaders may not have time to stop and think, sothey at least need help on the hoof.

Won't it sort itself out organically ? The consequences of closing our eyes and hoping for the best are too dangerous. Accountability structures already suggest that the system has no faith in its schools. Shallow structural policy-making has not dug the deep foundations necessary for stability and trust. We need to open our eyes, take a deep breath and restate our fundamental, vocational principles.

This book isn't an answer to the postmodern conundrum, but it might help us protect children from too much turbulence and uncertainty while the new system settles down into the reliable predictability that is the foundation for the best schools. It might be good that no one's telling us what to think any more, but we're all clever people and we should, in a self-improving school-led system, expect the best thinking of each other.

The nation trusts us to form young people. The taxpayer expects us to know what kind of example we should set them, but do we? How do we know what's right or wrong? New school structures mean that the model of the headteacher as a public intellectual, known and trusted in every community, isn't as clear as it was. It may be that the public finds it hard to understand new structures and it might look as if Ofsted, Ofqual and the Department for Education regulate as if they can't trust school leaders. It's sad to see public scandals about money, fraud and ego bringing school leadership into disrepute, and sadder still to see the endless false starts while education policy serves partisan political agendas. Losing public confidence is disastrous for the young we care for, so it has to be worth attempting to hold each other to high standards of conduct better than we do at the moment.

All school leaders paid by the taxpayer are public servants, and colleagues in independent schools serve their communities. We are not only expected to lead our schools but also to model something precious and good for the future so that young people may not just understand the world but also change it for the better.

We have highly complex professional duties and the ethical decisions we make – to do the right thing, to achieve a good result – are of enormous significance to the development of young people and society. We face ethical dilemmas every day. We talk them through with colleagues, governing boards, sometimes with parents and our communities, but we have no national framework that allows us to explore and test dilemmas against a set of ethical principles, no safe space in which to reflect.

Thinking school leaders should want to be clear about our educational endeavour. What do we do? Why do we do it? Who do we do it for? How should we do it? How do we tell right from wrong?

Returning to Ginger, headteachers have to do two things at once. First, to be good public servants carrying out our roles with energy and expertise. Second, to model the best of human behaviour to children so that they learn how to live well. I hope this book will help you do both of those, and give you a way to think that helps you be what you want to be: a force for good in society.

# 2 The Framework for Ethical Educational Leadership 2018

I used to work at a school on a former coalfield, both of which were struggling. We were considerably undersubscribed so the head told us all to talk the school up, not down, locally. I don't know if he included the gigantic graffito on the shopping centre that informed the citizenry 'Stevens is a fat bastard'. Stevens was a magnificent History teacher, a local councillor, a learned, kind and witty man. He could quash a gathering with a raised eyebrow and was reputed to greet new classes with 'My name's Stevens, and you all know what I am'. Whether we talked the school up or down was neither here nor there to those who knew the skills and motivation of the longest-serving teachers. There's no fancy management style or sloganeering that replaces trust in personalities in a small community. You wouldn't choose the graffito, but money couldn't buy what it, bizarrely, represented.

Running a school is both utterly predictable and fiendishly random. While the range of dilemmas a leader might tackle in the course of a day, a week, a year, even a career are generally in the same field, dealing with children, families, teachers and government are human interactions concerning love, hope and service. Such matters cannot be codified, even if you wanted to. They must be encountered and comprehended in the old-fashioned sense of being understood and tackled successfully. I talk about the different way of tackling ethics in later chapters but that will not lead to a natty little algorithm to solve them. We will have to think hard. I'm sorry if this is a blow.

What is offered, however, should be supportive and useful. School leaders face ethical dilemmas which worry us. What we need is the human equivalent of an algorithm: language, training and structure. This chapter is about the language which is helpful when thinking about ethical issues. This way, I hope that the encountering of dilemmas can be explained as central to our work.

There's much more on the background to these words later in the book, but setting them out now should help you think your way into the language of ethics and realise that it is everyday language for everyday issues, soul-searching as they may be.

**The Framework for Ethical Educational Leadership** was designed by the **Ethical Leadership Commission** 2017–2018.

*Ethical educational leadership is based upon the Seven Principles for Public Life.*

**1    Selflessness**

Leaders should act solely in the interest of children and young people.

**2    Integrity**

Leaders must avoid placing themselves under any obligation to people or organisations that might try inappropriately to influence them in their work. Before acting or taking decisions, they must declare and resolve openly any perceived conflict of interest and relationships.

**3    Objectivity**

Leaders must act and take decisions impartially and fairly, using the best evidence and without discrimination or bias. Leaders should be dispassionate, exercising judgement and analysis for the good of children and young people.

**4    Accountability**

Leaders are accountable to the public for their decisions and actions and must submit themselves to the scrutiny necessary to ensure this.

**5    Openness**

Leaders should act and take decisions in an open and transparent manner. Information should not be withheld from scrutiny unless there are clear and lawful reasons for so doing.

**6    Honesty**

Leaders should be truthful.

**7    Leadership**

Leaders should exhibit these principles in their own behaviour. They should actively promote and robustly support the principles and be willing to challenge poor behaviour wherever it occurs. Leaders include both those who are paid to lead schools and those who volunteer to govern them.

*Schools and colleges serve children and young people and help them grow into fulfilled and valued citizens. As role models for the young, how we behave as leaders is as important as what we do. Leaders should show leadership through the following personal characteristics or virtues.*

a    **Trust:** *leaders are trustworthy and reliable.* We hold trust on behalf of children and should be beyond reproach. We are honest about our motivations.

b **Wisdom:** *leaders use experience, knowledge and we demonstrate moderation and self-awareness.* We act calmly and rationally. We serve our schools and colleges with propriety and good sense.

c **Kindness***: leaders should demonstrate respect, generosity of spirit, understanding and good temper.* We give difficult messages humanely where conflict is unavoidable.

d **Justice:** *leaders are fair and work for the good of all children.* We seek to enable all young people to lead useful, happy and fulfilling lives.

e **Service:** *leaders are conscientious and dutiful.* We demonstrate humility and self-control, supporting the structure, conventionsand rules which safeguard quality. Our actions protect high-quality education.

f **Courage:** *leaders should work courageously in the best interests of children and young people.* We protect their safety and their right to a broad, effective and creative education. We hold one another to account courageously.

g **Optimism:** *leaders should be positive and encouraging.* Despite difficulties and pressures, we are developing excellent education to change the world for the better.

# Part I
# Professional school leaders

# 3 The headteacher as professional

As a newly qualified teacher in 1983 I didn't have a tutor group of my own in the very large comprehensive school in which I served. On Thursdays I had a morning duty at the entrance of one of the blocks where I was expected to supervise behaviour as classes gathered for morning registration. A nightmare duty in many ways, too vague to be understood by a beginner and requiring the corridor presence of an old hand. My Thursdays were made materially harder by an experienced colleague who turned up late to tutor time every week, and abandoned the form early to dismiss themselves and roam about. In a supervision session with the deputy head who was professional tutor to new teachers, I raised this matter and asked for advice. He didn't offer any but gave the colleague some pretty trenchant advice on her behaviour and how to put it right. Sure enough, next Thursday she advised me in turn with some asperity, accusing me of unprofessional behaviour and warning me to watch my step in future.

You might have gathered that the injustice of this still nibbles at me. I phoned my mother, a teacher for years, and asked what this 'professionalism' meant. Though sympathetic, she was a bit vague and suggested that she probably meant that I should have mentioned it to her first, rather than a deputy head. Fair point.

This little incident that probably only I remember illuminates our consideration of professionalism in teaching. I think that when teachers talk about 'acting professionally' it is a mixture of collegiality (don't tell tales to management), diligence-and-capability (do the job well) and confidentiality (be careful with what you know about children and their families). It glues a workforce together, but it's not professionalism.

Incidentally, the second time I was called unprofessional was 30 years later when a fellow head furiously accused me − erroneously − of telling a candidate about a confidential verbal reference he'd offered. He was wrong, but it was a better use of the word.

School leaders play a vital role in society. Their status is as **professionals** but what does that mean? This chapter discusses what we understand by professional behaviour.

## Is professionalism the same as leadership?

The term 'professionalism' is widely used by teachers and school leaders. The search for proper professional status has been subject to much agonising and the goal of groupings from the professional associations and trade unions through the old National College for School Leadership to the Department for Education. Have we made progress?

The furious parent dodging civilities at the gate is looking for a professional encounter. He knows that if he goes to a doctor, a lawyer or a priest, he'll be treated respectfully and listened to. He's not that certain about the reception he'll get from the headteacher. That's partly to do with his own experience of education, which might have been particularly bruising, and partly to do with the overwhelming force of the love he has for his child. Is his scepticism justified?

The *Teachers' Standards*, where leaders begin, are clear on the skills and abilities teachers should have but rather vague on ethical behaviour, aspects of right and wrong:

> A teacher is expected to demonstrate consistently high standards of personal and professional conduct . . . Teachers uphold public trust in the profession and maintain high standards of ethics and behaviour within and outside school.

The *National Standards of Excellence for Headteachers* (an interesting title in itself) cover similar ground:

> Headteachers occupy an influential position in society and shape the teaching profession. They are lead professionals and significant role models within the communities they serve. Headteachers, together with those responsible for governance, are guardians of the nation's schools.

Headteachers:

1   Hold and articulate clear values and moral purpose, focused on providing a world-class education for the pupils they serve.

2   Demonstrate optimistic personal behaviour, positive relationships and attitudes towards their pupils and staff, and towards parents, governors and members of the local community.

3   Lead by example – with integrity, creativity, resilience, and clarity – drawing on their own scholarship, expertise and skills, and that of those around them.

(Department for Education 2015a: 4)

Excellent sentiments, but what do they actually mean? For example, what are the component parts of a 'world-class education'? Good PISA scores by any means necessary? Doing it like they do it in Shanghai? What does resilience actually mean? Is it always desirable?

In recent years much has been written on school leadership and for good reason. It helps people reflect on their role and potentially acts as a sensible counterpoint to common character traits heads bring with them. These might include confidence, intelligence, dominance, articulacy and belief in the rightness and universability of one's own views. All good heads have these traits in greater or lesser form: the job would not be possible or attractive without them. Leadership training helps heads to work out how to use their particular combination of these traits to for the greater good. The trouble with some school leadership discourse, however, is that it brings with it a temptation for heads to be entirely self-referential and has overemphasised personal performance over *thinking*. This is particularly dangerous in a deregulated system where every school leader is potentially his own, autonomous, decision-maker

The story of the super- and individually lauded heads publicly praised by politicians and whose actions created the climate of 'strong leadership' in the early years of the 21st century needs to be told elsewhere. The consequent damage done to school leaders' collective reputation by some of their actions has been painful. Tabloids of all stripes archive stories about fraud, nepotism, bullying, cheating and eye-watering salaries paid from the public purse.

School leaders have perhaps been too polite or too busy keeping their own schools afloat to try to address the actions of notorious colleagues. Worryingly, we may also have been too afraid. If one criticises the outcomes or the methods of a noted colleague or blows a whistle on behaviour which lurches from strong to wrong, might that draw fire to oneself? If I say that she cheats to get results, might inspectors appear in *my* car park? If that happens, will it go well? Will governors lose confidence in me so I lose my job? What might such thought processes do to ethical thinking?

If a school is to run effectively and provide a safe and secure experience for children, then the job should, of course, be done briskly and with conviction. But this comes as a result of experience, reflection and intellectual capacity. Being 'strong' is a product of quality and experience, not just a personal choice. Quality and experience are fundamental to sound ethical decision-making: self-belief is not enough.

## What is a professional?

There is no common shared description of a professional, but we can probably take it to mean a well-educated worker engaged in an intellectually challenging role for which specific, difficult, regulated qualifications serve as an entry point. A professional might also be expected to demonstrate particular knowledge and skills, to keep those up-to-date and to engage in training and development. They may also have codes of conduct or agreed standards of behaviour, protected and upheld by associations. These protect the profession's integrity, preventing it from becoming diluted or being brought into disrepute. Wider society generally knows what to expect of a professional, and a profession knows what it expects of itself; it will have a shared purpose.

Teaching and school leadership has, historically, not had such a structure. We have traditionally been a centralised workforce, part of both local and national government, not independent. We have heretofore been highly unionised. Lately, outcomes alone have been used as a measure of educators' worth. The government commissions and regulates teachers, the unions protect teachers and in between are school leaders, risen through the ranks, who try to make the teaching workforce meet the commissioners' demands. While leaders are undoubtedly qualified to the level of other professionals, there is a dissonance in independence and self-understanding between, for example, us and the medics.

In the next section I will try to unpick some of their practices to see if they will help us.

## The nature of professionalism

School leaders are prone to lament that they have to fulfil all the roles of all other professionals in their daily work. That is hyperbolic, but it will help us to look at three different professions and try to use some more linguistic scaffolding, armed with which we can explore the professional practices of school leaders.

We can start with a simple definition. **Professionals** work in the best interests of their patient or client. A professional's intervention into the life of another person is done with permission and agreement, and with the intention that the result is better for the beneficiary.

### Medicine

Doctors share a broad approach to their medical profession which is based on the 'Hippocratic Oath' – part of fourth- and fifth-century BC medical writings in Greek. This ancient underpinning of the profession manages the power that doctors have, particularly with their patients. Versions of the oath include duties to:

- Help the sick, according to their ability and judgement; and not to injure or do wrong.

- Know the limits of what they can do and refer to others who could help.

- Keep confidential what they are told or find out in the course of their treatment.

- Look after their teacher and pass their knowledge on.

- Avoid using their access to a private house as an opportunity for wrongdoing.

Doctors experience ethics as a STOP sign. Medical ethics discusses **consent**: where a patient has a possible treatment explained to them and they agree, after consideration, to have the treatment, or decide not to. In legal terms, not having consent to carry out a treatment can be seen as an assault on a sick person.

Medicine is also controlled by the law of the land. Doctors are constrained not to do various actions by the prevailing national legal code, no matter what they might think or be able to do with the patient's consent. **Constraint** takes ethics beyond an individual professional into wider society.

But the medical profession is a good thing. Doctors bring their **expertise** to the sick and vulnerable. They have special knowledge which can save and transform lives through their analysis, argument, planning and practical skill.

The duty of doctors to care and heal brings us help and benefits which it is hard to imagine life without. The **benefit** of medicine is clear in every experience of pain ended and life lengthened.

## Law

The organisation of seeking justice and administering the law deals with conflicts and disagreements. These may be painful and emotional, ambiguous and grasping. The law manages the arguments and disagreements by setting up complementary roles and responsibilities.

A client goes to a solicitor for help with making an argument. The solicitor may be asked to send an agreed letter and this acts as a force on behalf of the client. The client may also not agree with the solicitor's advice. In other cases, a solicitor may be the person who acts as an intermediary for a client's money, because they are known to be trustworthy, to pass it to another person. Like the doctor there is **consent** between the client and professional.

Law is in part about how society constrains and restricts what we can do. The professional relationship is controlled both by the professional body's rules and the law of the jurisdiction. For example, lawyers must work within the structure of the law. **Constraint** also restricts who can act and speak in particular settings: a solicitor can't speak in a higher court; it has to be a barrister.

The **expertise** of the lawyer is what the client pays for. They know the law and can write or talk quicker and more succinctly with greater precision that an amateur.

The **benefit** to the client is seen in the resolution of a dispute, the sorting out of a muddle, or the establishment of a new piece of work or relationship.

Of course the law is not as simple as this. A professional in the police service may seek consent, but may not get it from a law breaker. They are then empowered to act on behalf of other people who might be at immediate or long-term risk. The power to arrest is given as a form of **consent** by society. The extent of the force that can be used is constrained. **Constraint** continues when the police put together a case for independent scrutiny and judgement in a court. Police officers have an

**expertise** in dealing with situations that the rest of us find frightening and unusual. It is also found in recognising and naming the links between the legal code and human behaviour. We **benefit** from the peace that is brought by the apprehension of wrongdoers and the benefits of a law-abiding society.

## Faith

The example of priests acting as professionals is illuminating for other reasons. Families and individuals **consent** to shape their own lives around ancient teachings and accept a level of interference in private decision-making. If they go further and ask for advice or develop their faith by specific teaching or social action projects, they consent at each point. The priest's **constraints** are canon law and the law of the land. The **expertise** of the priest is seen in their transmission of the memory of human spirituality stretching back many generations and linking to human experiences of life now. Religious people may **benefit** by a sense of peace, being part of a wider trusted community, or by working on a project to improve the world, which they could not do alone.

But priests know that we do not live in a theocracy where one form of religion is dominant and legitimate. Catholic Spain's Inquisition and John Knox's Scotland are no more. A single system, a Magisterium of faith, is far from our experience in Britain. Our world of meanings is postmodern, in the sense that there are lots of stories with different emphases. I might choose to go to that priest, or why not the Iman, or the yoga class, or a Jungian counsellor, or maybe just go for a nice paddle with a kayak club? I have alternative ways in which to form my cosmic view.

## How does this help build our professionalism as a headteacher?

With no great subtlety I have characterised aspects of professionalism to encourage us to analyse school leadership using four broad themes. Two might be described as the brake and two as the accelerator. I will use these to give some shape and regularity to the questions we want to answer for a complex role.

We will look at:

1   **Consent**: who decides and who agrees with what is being done? How do we know?

2   **Constraint:** what laws and rules stop some actions and decisions? Are we at peace with the constraints?

3   **Expertise:** what is expertise? Knowledge and curriculum? Management and money? Community building? Innovation or transmission?

4   **Benefit:** who benefits? What if there is a clash between stakeholders' benefits?

But these themes on their own won't help clarify what we are trying to do. When you begin to consider the stakeholders in a school there are usually at least three very different groups:

a  **The children and young people**

b  **The parents of the pupils**

c  **Society beyond the school**

The analysis of what is a professional approach needs to be complete and fair to each of these before we begin to balance and negotiate interests.

Finally, the question of post- modernism adds a further twist to any analysis. We might say that *modern* organisation in education emphasises the use of the same components and processes. English educators might once have joked that education in France was so nationally coordinated that a school in Auxerre and another in Bordeaux would be teaching the same subject at the same point in the week with the same materials and the same pedagogy. English education was rarely one approach. Current policy has let a thousand flowers bloom, each with its own ethos, curriculum emphasis and pedagogical combinations.

In the next chapters I'll apply consent, constraint, expertise and benefit to school leadership as we work with parents, children and society to see if this helps us devise an ethical routemap. What are we doing, why and how? And how do we match up to Kipling's old observation?

No printed word nor spoken plea can teach young minds what they should be.

Not all the books on all the shelves – but what the leaders are themselves.

# The professional for the child

Many years ago I went one Friday to pick up my son from Reception. We were off to stay with family and he'd hoped to take reading books for the journey and to show Gran (another teacher). On emerging he seemed dissatisfied so we went to talk to Mrs Anson. She listened to him and picked up a box of books. She tipped it out onto the floor with 'You're quite capable, pick as many as you like'. He studied the pile, selected three and showed her. She nodded and said he could read them to her on Monday. He tucked them under a small arm, she smiled politely at me and we were dismissed. The transaction was entirely between teacher and child, dealt with at his level and for his benefit. While I wanted to show off to my mother how quickly he was making progress, Mrs Anson wanted him to accept responsibility as a reader on that day, in that place, independent of my ambitions for him. That teacher superbly represented the state's aims for education to me and my boy. It was a revelatory moment for me.

This chapter will focus on school leaders as professionals who work for the benefit of children and young people. We'll walk around the place and value of young people in society and our professional work. We'll walk around schools as places where children are guarded and valued and some of the professional tensions affecting our work. Towards the end I'll kick the four tyres I fitted earlier. How does consent work? What constraints apply? What expertise do we bring? How does the young person benefit from our work?

Schools are full of children. They're everywhere, impeding the progress of adult public servants through the corridors of the buildings we put up to house them. From the 5-year-old on a mission, to the 18-year-old slouching towards Gov and Pol, they expect to be served, protected and not a little irritated by the system put up to develop them. We spend a huge amount of public money on them and we agonise about it all the time. A small minority of parents add to their tax expenditure by paying for education apart from the crowd, so worried are they about the effect that the wrong sort of schooling might have on the beloved child. Others are only prepared to have him or her taught by the religion of the home, such might be the spiritual damage of thoughtless education. This delicate creature must have a value beyond rubies, to be so worried over. What is it?

Schools are where society chooses to look after its young through the prolonged childhood and adolescence of the human being. Humans take a long time to complete their physical and cognitive growth. Over centuries in the west we've decided to educate children formally so that they know enough stuff to be useful to the community and are able to tackle the world independently. We know how to keep them alive at and beyond birth, we don't use them as slave labour, we tend not to have manual or production-line jobs to which education is irrelevant, and we're a bit more queasy about sending millions of them to die in battle. Significantly, since relatively recently, we educate girls as well as boys and don't expect them to spend lives of quiet domesticity.

There is precious little in our national life or system about the value of the child. We take it for granted that children need to be loved, that they should be protected, and that upon their fruitfulness rests the future health of the nation. A child gone wrong is potentially a wasted life and a useless, helpless, perhaps dangerous, citizen.

Dunford's review (2010) of the Office of the Children's Commissioner alluded to this problem as he sought to clarify the purpose of the role.

> I have been represented with many reasons why children and young people need someone with statutory backing to promote and protect their interests. The most compelling are that
>
> ▪ Children and young people are more vulnerable to human rights violations than adults
>
> ▪ Children's needs and interests are often not on the radar of policy formers and decision makers and are usually given lower priority than the needs and interests of adults
>
> ▪ They do not have the same means as adults to bring about systemic change through voting or taking part in the political process
>
> ▪ They usually find it more difficult than adults to access the judicial system or use other legal means of redress.
>
> (Dunford 2010: 10)

Dunford's conclusion (among others) is that the Children's Commissioner's most important job is to 'promote and protect the rights of children as set out in the UNCRC' (Dunford 2010, rec 1.6, p20).

Later in the book we'll consider the United Nations Convention on the Rights of the Child. It sets out – wonderfully – the rights of the child, but not why they should have them. Perhaps that is expected to be understood from the adult declaration on human rights, that all should be treated with dignity, equality, granted freedoms and protections and so on, but while necessary, it is insufficient. It is too short a step from protecting children's rights so that they may flourish as adults and help build a better world, to seeing the first 18 years of life as just a waiting room. That's no help to school leaders. Our responsibility to children is only partially so that they might be useful and happy adults. Our presenting responsibility is so that they may be useful and happy *children.*

So this chapter looks at our professional relationship to the child as child. What is her value, now? How is this realised in the education we offer?

## The value of the child

Kant said that making children's lives bearable was a necessary consequence of the act of procreation (Kant 1996:64). If you want the sex, you'd better look after the children. That marked a change in the way people thought about the young, from poorly formed things who needed, perhaps literally, beating into shape to be adults appropriate to their station, to being a gift valuable in themselves, worthy of a good life, themselves. From this start, western liberals started to consider what education children needed or should have, and how they developed physically and mentally. Schools therefore exist for the benefit of the children. We have schools because we want to do something good for all children as they grow up.

This took a very long time. While churches and some charitable foundations grasped the need to educate especially boy-children, the purpose of that education was functionalist. Schools set up in the late Middle Ages and into modern times to educate the poor or the rich did so according to the norms of the day. If an educated man needed to be able to brandish Latin and Greek and a little mathematics, that was what was taught. Theology, Natural Science and much later, History, were added to the curriculum and battle-lines are still drawn around those older prejudices. When girls began to be educated, it was also for usefulness in many guises: to be 'accomplished' in a drawing room, useful in a kitchen or factory as directed by men; her father, brothers, employer or foreman.

It took several generations to implement the 1870 Education Act effectively and build up both the teaching profession and satisfactory curricula for 5 to 11-year-olds. There were several false starts in establishing universal secondary schooling, and only recently have we committed to ensuring learning for the whole of the legal age of childhood up to 18 (despite our still compulsorily examining them at 16 as if they could leave then).

In the middle part of the last century some educators sought to resist the functional and develop so-called child-centred education, immoderately rubbished in our national discourse. Whether this was sensible or not is a battle long gone: politics requires education to be at its service, an arena in which promises about the economic future may be made and measured. We still educate for functionalist reasons, but we also belong to a society which wants every child to be well educated, and we look out to a world where other governments are trying to extend education to all parts of the young population: beyond 11, to girls as well as boys. 200 years ago small children worked under cotton looms and agile ones were sent up chimneys or down mines: the very existence of compulsory education through-out childhood is evidence of our valuing the child, a public good.

Educators of all stripes talk about children's development. Given the chance, any one of them will tell you that education comes from the Latin root *educare*, to draw out, to make the child the best she can be. Some go further to say that educa-tion needs to be inserted or transmitted, and some that it needs to be encouraged and uncovered. All will hope that the education favoured by the institution under advisement will lay the foundation for a learned and useful adult, a worker, a cit-izen, a parent, a leader. This ground is hotly disputed, but all of us are partially right. The reason we can't agree about what we think schools are for is that we don't really know what we think about children. If we could arrive at an under-standing of the value of the child, then we'd have more of a chance of knowing what schools should do and how they should be led.

Let us try to get past the limitations of the system. For reasons of efficiency we have to educate *en masse*, in herds. The education we offer is a mixture of:

- what we think is right;

- what we can prove to be useful;

- what the nation values;

- what we can afford.

The children come to schools with the full range of aptitudes, characteristics and human needs. Generally speaking, for excellent reasons of justice and fairness, we educate them altogether. For utilitarian and economic reasons the personal tailoring the system can offer is limited so schools do the best they can within the four drivers listed above. The educated young human at the end of it has output measures of his skills against what society values.

So, the developing child is necessarily put to the purposes of the taxpayers' education system. If the average child may achieve x or y then it is said to be good for the nation (if not for mathematics) that all children at least attain this reason-able expectation. If they do not, then the education system must be made to enable them. At times of limited public spending, this is more cheaply done through exhortation than investment. Schools 'let children down' or 'condemn them to live within the circumstances of their birth' when an individual child falls short of the calibration set to measure the herd. Teachers are castigated and heads roll. A good education which prepares children for adult life is understood to be progress along the path laid out by government and educators, as well as possible at the time.

Children, however, are not just human beings in waiting but human beings themselves. They are born human and retain that humanity until they die. They are human at all points of life. They are not more human at 18 than at 6 or 13, nor is the child who understands the world through mathematics more human than one who understands it through football. The child who enjoys herd education and the child who loathes it are equally human. A kind child and a cruel one are both human. A beautiful child with four A levels is no more or less human than a truanting urchin with an aggressive hairdo.

We fail them all if we see them as performance-fodder, and we have come too close to that in recent times. When education's schools are judged entirely by the output measures of the day, reflecting the politico-economic hopes of the era, children who succeed in the system become trophies validating the system. Others become whatever is the opposite of a trophy: a failure, an also-ran, a disregarded nothing. Encouraged by the state to understand child development through the lens of the education system, parents also pressure them to achieve 'beyond expectations' so that their child, their own beloved, will be valued by the state and its pundits and their parenting endorsed. Some children rise to it, some fail, some rebel. Some take their own lives rather than fail the expectations of the family and the state.

(That the end point of schooling in England uses a gold-standard measure originally designed as a university entrance examination for a tiny minority of privileged young people with an aptitude for book-learning probably means that we are doomed to gold-plate the failures of the past until we can think up a gateway to adult life with universal applicability. That's a matter outside this book's scope.)

The context in which I write has proved materially detrimental to the health of our young. That some are stressed to death by the need to achieve what society values and their families have been taught to value is only part of the tragedy. Educational functionalism combined with the commodification of the young means that adults are distant from children. Economic necessity forces parents to work long hours: what they buy, including what they buy for their children, is what the market requires, and it services children's independence.

So what is the value of the child in society? We value what they might become and what they might offer us economically. We haven't yet found a way of valuing every child in the present moment, as the vulnerable young of the species. Perhaps we could start with these principles?

- Adults choose to have children.

- The child is a citizen of equal value to the adult.

- Children can't meet their own needs. They rely on adults.

- The covenant adults enter into is to love and care for children as they grow and develop.

- The welfare of children is the test of society's integrity. Where children are well looked after, the people flourish.

Yes, we need to teach them what they need to survive and prosper; yes, we need an educated workforce; yes, every child should learn to love the consolations of literature and the excitement of science; yes, we need a way of monitoring the success of our schools. These are righteous activities, but they need the present good of the child at their centre. Do our activities make children's lives bearable now, as children? Kant deserves an answer.

## Schools and their adults

In our society we professionalise what we value, which explains the immense amount of education and adherence to codes of ethics we require in our doctors, lawyers and priests. It might sensibly be argued that if our children are more important than anything else – and which good parent would say otherwise? – we should be very careful, fastidious and demanding about how we educate, train and value those to whom we entrust children for so many years. It is hard to reconcile that with the current vogue for politically responsive, cheap, on-the-job, quickly promoted, school-based teacher training where craft skills are allegedly learned the hard way, reflection isn't done in the firm's time and behaviour management – one of the most-admired skills of teachers – is someone else's problem.

How does this work for our children? The obvious criticism is that teachers should be qualified in a manner that has been refined over many years independent of the political timetables, that those who will care for our children should be trained thoroughly, that a busy school does not necessarily offer the chance to ingest the distinguished academic disciplines of child development and education, and that the craft skills take years and wisdom to accumulate. The care of our young should be entrusted to those who themselves possess what society values: much learning, astounding interpersonal skills and professional status. Why is a teacher less valued than a dentist?

The answer takes us once again back to the value of the child. Other professionals have a direct and valued impact on adults' lives: on their health, their liberty, their money, their homes, their teeth. Educators deal with children. They can't vote and they don't have much cash. They behave in ways we don't like in adults: they're needy, tedious, ungrateful, awkward, self-obsessed, embarrassing, even dangerous. They're not very strong for many years and they need an unconscionable amount of food and sleep. They stop adults from pleasing themselves. They're easy (ish) to quash and it's not entirely illegal to hit them. They need a lot of time, and that's at a bit of a premium. You don't need to be able to present a set of accounts or argue a case in the Supreme Court to be able to look after a child. You don't need any qualifications at all to be a parent. Therefore, those who are entrusted with parenting on the state's behalf can be dismissed as inferior to other more adult-important professions. You'll have heard it said : 'Those who can, do. Those who can't, teach.'

This is not the place for a description of the different kinds of teacher training in the educational jurisdictions of the world, nor how the UK's matches their standards. My point is simple: schools are the universal service as far as children are concerned. From starting to leaving school there is a state-appointed parent attached to a child. If we really valued children, we'd want to make sure that those paradigm parents were selected by the most competitive processes, trained intensely and lengthily to a very high level, held to the standards and in the respect we accord to other professionals. The teacher pipeline should be strictly and efficiently controlled and their working conditions should be such that they are enabled to progress through stringent in-service qualifications and refresher training so that quality may reasonably be guaranteed. Such accountability should be endemic in the system not based on political whim, but on what the nation desires, after careful thought, for all its children.

School leaders, who ensure the quality and tone of each institution, should reasonably expect to be subject to intense screening and scrutiny of their actions and motivations as well as their examination metrics. The paradigm parent is the uber-parent, the ur-parent, the parent who has devoted his adult life to learning what will benefit children most and making it happen in schools. **'Those who can, teach.'**

I discuss *in loco parentis* in terms of our relationship with parents in the next chapter, but its responsibilities should inform the educator's every action. We should aim for a paradigm of parenting where the school is focused on the child and is a guarantor of his rights and protections, as well as whatever calibration the state deems necessary. It is not enough that a child should be qualified, but she should also be developing agency, reflecting on life and how best to live it, encountering and learning the values that build up our common life. Therefore, schools' responsibility as the state's paradigm parents for 15,000 hours should be built on a secure ethical code. How might we arrive at that?

Let us return to the four tests of professionalism that I suggested earlier. How are we professionals for the child? What do we hope children will get from our leadership of its schools?

## Consent

Consent and young people is a famous area of ethical subtlety. We try to assess what this looks like in their sex lives using the ironically named 'Gillick competences'. Some European states look askance at our willingness to find under-18s guilty of crimes, or capable of military training.

When a child enters a secondary school they are well on the way to being adults. By the time they are 18 they need to be independent and able to decide for themselves (unless there is a precise statement of why their support should continue to 25). The Scout Association has used an effective diagram of the extent of adult decision-making compared with the child. It is a simple rectangle with a diagonal from one corner to the other. As the child grows from 0 (when they are completely dependent on adults) to 18 (when they become an adult), the amount of adult intervention tapers away to nothing.

We know this in our practice as educators. We no longer beat knowledge into pupils, or rely on rote learning. We want to develop people with a love of reading. We like curious practical enquirers who make a difference in the world by thinking things through. We want to equip and inspire lifelong learners with grounding in subjects which they will build on throughout their lives. Consent is the key to all these goals. Children choose to spend time discovering, exploring and becoming expert in subjects they like.

Joy and fulfilment found in learning is part of each young person's own individual development. In the UK particularly, we understand the rich contribution that individual creativity and ground-breaking intelligence can bring to human civilisation. While it's fun to mock the old school report of a famous musician, artist, inventor or writer, most schools want their young people to find their passion and métier and encourage them when they do.

We live in a complex society with interconnected areas of work, which we rely on. The health service needs nurses; we all do. Advice and guidance about how a young person is doing at school needs to be not just given but engaged with by the pupil because the stakes are high for everyone. Yes, do a job with joy, but do a job where your work is valuable to all of us.

We can risk functionalism when we talk about employment in school. But the long fight against NEETs (those Not in Education Employment or Training) has been about fighting lifelong poverty. Poverty is personally and socially disastrous, reducing life expectancy and wasting precious human resources. Somehow, the young people need to spot the risk and consent to learning rather than falling into poverty and poor work.

In fact, schools are places where young people develop their capacity to say yes to opportunities, their growth and a place in wider society. They train to be fit enough to be picked for a team. They study to push the boundaries of mathematics. They practise instruments. They try out talking in new languages. They write. They take part in restorative justice projects. They volunteer. When a school runs well, children's consent is given freely as they participate in the norms and riches of community life.

When we act as professionals in school we try to get young people to consent to what is going on, to use their own resources and capacities to enhance their lives. Unlike the doctor, the decision-making isn't usually done in a crisis. The school-life timescale is long and careful. Great schools see young people take more and more independent decisions about making the best of their lives the older they get. Getting consent, through engagement, is vital.

## Constraint

Because children are vulnerable we manage what we do to protect their best interests. We have responded to the abuse of children over 50 years, we have clarified what we expect of education, and we have developed our schools as the safe place in all children's lives as they grow up.

Our first constraint is to keep children and young people safe. The law protects children and young people from harm, and there are systems to back up our work to keep young people safe. We no longer keep physical punishment books because we do not beat children as part of school discipline. Since the 1996 Dunblane shootings, school buildings are built with secure perimeters and manageable entrances. We record bullying and racist incidents and need to deal with them. Since the Soham killings, we use the Disclosure and Barring Service (DBS) to check potential employees against national information about people convicted, or cautioned, about offences against people who therefore might (on the balance of probability) pose a safety risk to our young people.

The Cullen Inquiry report (1996) drew attention to the weakness of public bodies in challenging Thomas Hamilton at a series of points in his life before he killed the 16 Dunblane primary school children and their teacher, wounding a further 10 pupils and 3 members of staff. The Bichard Inquiry (2004) showed clearly that several public bodies had evidence of behaviour by Ian Huntley that suggested he posed a risk to young women. If these had been shared within a circle of professional cooperation the pattern of his behaviour could have been noticed and, perhaps, the deaths of two girls avoided. Our constraints to safeguard our young people inherit these insights. We need to challenge behaviour we think is a risk. We work with partners to check properly and share relevant information – both nationally with the DBS, and locally with partners we know and see. These constraints protect our young people.

Our second area of constraint is time. More effective large data sets have set up challenges to schools about what they do with the young people while they are at school. League tables are based on the progress made in learning and being assessed publicly. This leads to the management questions about the inputs in terms of time and resources.

Each school year has 190 days with about 1,000 hours of learning a year. Securing each child's full entitlement to the precious taught hours, which are also the biggest school budget item, is the job of every head. It's why we need high attendance, why family holidays in term time are such a risk for children and why we need to be careful about inventing out-of-lesson tasks which amuse us. We know how learners long to flee from subjects they find hard. But it is our job to defend the (limited) hours carved out of national taxes and to present timetabled care to each of our young people.

A third constraint is what can be called the reproduction of social exclusion. Will our young people live the same constrained lives their parents do? Do we run a school for an estate, or ghetto which no one ever leaves? Birmingham City Council showed great leadership in education when they devised entitlements for their children and young people. They stretched the experiences of all young people by expecting them to explore the city and the world, with a widening circle of places to go and things to do as they grow.

In the research and debates about young people's social inclusion and social mobility, one of the key characteristics of effective social organisations is the achievement of 'bridging social capital'. In school this means meeting people not like us, going to places and having experiences we don't normally have. Research in this area can pose stark challenges. The National Trust reviewed who benefits from their work, and found they were weak at including BAME people. They try now to see how they can improve. What does it take, when most live in towns and cities, to visit the Lake District fells? Where are the opportunities in a school? Where do your young people go?

## Expertise

We bring expertise to our young people. We provide the subject knowledge they need to engage with the National Curriculum, the exam syllabus, and the transmitted and renewing wisdom of humanity.

We have our subject specialisms. It's pretty frustrating for a timetabler to include the head who is too often off to meetings, dealing with parents, dealing with teachers; and so needs cover. But it's a reminder of the core task of a school and a demonstration that what each teacher does is not trivial. We can share our love of subject knowledge and model an adult who learns and shares that learning.

We recruit a team of teachers to cover the whole curriculum. What is the best we can achieve? Will we set a threshold of a top university degree in the right subject? How will we select from the actual candidates who come for interview? How can we help a struggling teacher review his choice? How can we be experts for the young person if we don't know the subject they want to learn?

We are experts in how to teach and we know a huge amount about pedagogy. We understand how to capture a child's attention and how to build up his knowledge and learning. We can coach them to pass an examination and we can sow the seeds for a lifelong fascination with a subject which might change the world.

We are experts in how to manage behaviour in small and large groups. We know how to be fair and how to impose our will on groups of young people who may well be bigger, faster and cleverer than us. We know when to be loud and when to be quiet, and we know when to hold the line so that children learn that actions have consequences. We can manage a classroom, a corridor, an assembly, a bus journey and a trip halfway across the world.

We are experts in caring for our young people, especially those on the edges of coping. Pastoral staff and systems are fast, responsive, thoughtful and effective. We have more control over manyyoung people than the police, the magistrates and their parents. Our expertise keeps them safe and teaches them what they need to know.

## Benefit

Finally, benefit. How does what we do benefit the child? This has nothing to do with external fripperies. What is his experience of school as part of life? Is she safe and happy?

Schools build communities in our school. Does every child belong and feel valued? Or do we put a premium on some types of behaviour and find others less likely to attract acceptance?

How well have we succeeded in helping a young person develop as a solid citizen of any age? It has nothing to do with the reputation of the school, inspection grade, the colour of the blazer or the state of the building. The benefit is what the child carries when she walks through the door to assume the mantle of adult society. It only has a little bit to do with examination grades, insofar as they may determine, for a short while, other doors though which she may pass.

Does our child know things that will help her? Can he now, in fact, learn and seek out learning for himself? When she gets new equipment, can she get it to work? When faced with a situation or phenomenon, can she analyse and respond? Does all that exam practice mean that he can express his learning concisely and with application?

Further, does she know what being a good person looks like? How well has that been modelled? School leaders perform two simultaneous functions when it comes to passing this benefit to children. They are both conduit and model: they must teach children how to be scholarly while being a model of scholarship themselves, and they must teach children how to be good while setting an example of goodness themselves. If they do not value learning, then it is unlikely that they will be able to pass on a love of learning to children. If they behave badly, then children see that power can be accrued by bad behaviour and hypocrisy. *Do as I say, kids, but not as I do.* Or: *do as you're told, without question. Don't bandy words with me, child, show some respect.* Respect for what?

Offering the benefit of the good role model is part of every action in a school, every system and process, official and unofficial that happens to the child. It looks like this in practice: before the average secondary scholar gets up close to Keats or Lovelace, she might have been conveyed on a school bus, hung about in a school yard or corridor for a bit, bonded with her form tutor and experienced an assembly. She may be dressed in a uniform and she might have had to line up or progress through a building according to fixed norms. If she feels unsafe or unhappy, there'll be someone to turn to and if she's naughty someone will put her right. Byron and Euclid won't get a look in until the psychologists, philosophers, sociologists, theologians and educationalists have patted her down, wound her up and pointed her in the right direction.

These norms are not universal but decreed by the head or enshrined in the tradition of the school. While they are usually similar: don't talk over the teacher, don't disrupt learning, do your homework, don't hit people, swear, push or run, respect the fabric of the building – there's no reason why they should be. Schools may also entertain all sorts of outré positions: always walk with your hands behind your back, don't dye your hair, call me Madam. That most schools run along broadly similar lines suggests that we might have a set of assumptions about what behaviour models benefit the young. Keep safe, be polite, try your best.

In order to demonstrate public benefit our scholar should, therefore, not only have the qualifications he needs clutched in his youthful paw, but be able to demonstrate what he learned from the character of the adults around him, selfless public servants modelling the best in character and virtue. Has he benefitted from clever teachers in happy communities with intellectual endeavour to nourish the developing brain and the attitudes to make the world a better place? The benefit a child deserves to derive from the professional school leader includes all of these: did he get his entitlement?

# 5 The professional for parents

## *In loco parentis* – 'in the position of a parent'

Let's catch up with the angry parent barging past the perky professional at the school gate. He was crossing a threshold not just of hope, but of responsibility. Outside school he is in charge of his child: once inside, someone else is, the school leader and the staff she deploys. The parent's cry of 'What's the school going to do about this?' really means 'Why aren't you doing what I would do? How did you let this happen? You're meant to look after my child so what kind of outfit is it that has so distressed her, my joy and delight?' He has a legitimate question under the anger and bluster, which is something like:

'I have as much a right as you to expect for my child that which you would expect for your own. As an informed person, you'd recognise and demand the best education for your little one. I'm not an informed person, so help me, would you? Make it better, get it right. If I'm expected to hand her over to you, look after her like I would, please.'

The relationship between parents and school is a tricky one. Once upon a time parents were discouraged from entering schools and those who wanted to engage might have had a struggle. More recently, schools and parents have tried to work closely together and it's a rare school that doesn't say that it is in partnership with parents, but what does that actually involve?

Home – School agreements may seem friendly but they are largely about schools delivering stated outcomes and services, and parents supporting the local methodology. Most go further and, in their behaviour policies or websites, enlist the help of parents in this development, through home – school contracts and other hopeful partnerships. Some take another step and seek to direct parents' parenting: homework, bedtimes, clean uniform, screen time and the like. Parents might be forgiven for thinking that despite the hours schools spend on engaging parents, when push comes to shove it all tends towards 'This is how we do things here.

Thank you in advance for your cooperation'. That some parents then resort to evasion or shouting is, perhaps, inevitable.

Schools' determination is not necessarily unreasonable. Schools aren't democracies and professionals must make judgements about the best way to care for children *in loco parentis*. What kind of partnership can parents expect? It may exacerbate matters that in a time of increased autonomy they all go about it a bit differently. Now that schools are structured so differently a grievance can't always be lobbed straight up to the County Hall. If it's hard to know where to make your howl of anguish into the management structure of the Multi-Academy Trust (MAT), what is our desperate or truculent parent to expect? What relationship based upon which values underpins the response of the school-as-parent to the angry father at the desk? We need to get to the personal attributes and guiding principles of the person who embodies the ethos of the school, the leader, and all those who lead.

Commenting on parenting is notoriously controversial. The concept of *in loco parentis* itself is based on the idea that there is potential agreement on what a good parent might want for a child, but the 1989 Elton Report into school discipline made a series of recommendations about parents which suggested a deficit. Elton said:

> The Government, LEAs, governors and headteachers should consider means of impressing upon parents that the ways in which they bring up their children are likely to have a significant effect on their behaviour in school. Parents should:
>
> ■ provide firm but affectionate guidance in the home, which is most likely to produce the attitudes on which good behaviour in school can be based;
>
> ■ ensure that they set a good and consistent example to their children by their own behaviour;
>
> ■ avoid permissive or harshly punitive responses to aggressive behaviour, particularly by boys, which can encourage attitudes which are incompatible with schooling.
>
> The Secretaries of State should ensure that education for parenthood is fully covered as a cross-curricular theme in the National Curriculum.
>
> (Elton 1989, Chapter 5, para 15, rec 68, p 136)

> Governors and headteachers should ensure that education for parenthood is fully covered in school personal and social education programmes.

> The Government should develop a post-school education strategy aimed at promoting socially responsible parenthood.

> Parents should take full advantage of all channels of communication made available by schools and develop good working relationships with teachers in order to help their children to become constructive members of the school community.

Parent-teacher associations should ensure that their activities are accessible and rewarding to as many parents as possible.

Parents should make every effort to attend parents' evenings and annual parents' meetings.

The Government should explore the possibilities for imposing on parents civil liability for their children's acts in school.

(Elton 1989, Chapter 5)

PM David Cameron got into hot water when he floated the idea of compulsory *'even aspirational'* parenting classes for all, not just the poor. In sharp contrast to Elton, Tom Bennet's 2017 review 'Creating a Culture' has no such recommendations, beyond implying that a school should set out its behavioural expectations clearly in advance, that social media might help communication with parents and that exclusion review panels should uphold schools' decisions.

Conscientious heads in areas where academic outcomes are stubbornly low have spent thousands of hours trying to work with parents who may be frightened of, indifferent or antagonistic towards schools, with varying degrees of success. In the years of Every Child Matters there was money for liaison staff, and the work of Children's Centres was designed to plug these anxious or angry parents into education from before the child's birth.

School leaders, however, serve the child in the moment and we cannot wait for long-term government projects to change people's lives – especially as projects stop when governments change. School leaders have to work with parents as they are.

Some children, from seriously dysfunctional or actively harmful families, have to be protected. There are formal safeguarding structures for that. There are informal mechanisms for others: a kind adult who offers a safe haven: a place with a shower and clean uniform; free places on school trips; housing support in the sixth form; breakfast, lunch and tea; a head of year's sleepless nights over what will happen when Petal leaves school, hoping that family failure won't be repeated in her own life, that the gods of employment and relationships will be kind. Schools have become skilled at recognising trauma as an effect of poor parenting and some even have this as an element of their policies.

There's an interesting patch of boggy ground between working with chaotic parents and putting secure structures around the child at school. Most schools skirt around it but some stride across it confidently. It's where professionals' hopes for the child's future generates comment on her present circumstances. A school driven by zeal to rescue children from generational poverty might couch aspirations thus. *If you work hard at school, you'll be successful. That way you can escape from the poverty in which you've grown and reap the benefits of prosperity.* Some schools spell those out: *nice car, good holidays, enough to look after your own children well.*

We need to be careful about a pernicious assumption that prosperity is a require-ment of the good life. While grinding poverty is a human tragedy and entrenched inequality a national disgrace, it is possible to be an excellent parent who hap-pens to be poor, a loving parent indifferent to examination results and a cruel or disastrous parent with a shiny Lexus and a house in the Dordogne. Wealth may be closely linked to achievement, but goodness is not linked to income. While it is right that schools use disadvantage funding to give poor children the pricey cul-tural proxies of the rich, we need to be clear that this particular attempt to change the world is about economic inequality, not innate human worth.

The boggiest part of the bog is the equation of poverty with wickedness or weak-ness. Let's imagine Mr Smith. He's been married for 20 years, has a nice car, a big mortgage and wants his daughter to be a doctor. Nearby, Ms Jones has chucked out the fathers of her children and often relies on the food bank. These are circum-stance, perhaps just luck. They tell us no more. But Mr Smith's daughter weeps alone in her en-suite bedroom for fear of failure while Ms Jones's boy mucks in with the little ones before he and his mum watch telly together on a battered sofa. When schools move from parenting the child in school today to judging parenting at home, we should make sure that we know what we value. Hatty has a stable fam-ily but Ryan needs a male role model, what exactly is it that we want modelling? Is it Mr Smith?

## Kicking the tyres: applying four tests of professionalism

Despite being on an east-facing hilltop in Durham, we cleared the children outside at lunchtime. One September Monday I'd chivvied everyone out and was enjoying an empty space with the doors open to the sunshine. Atrociously, a Year 11 boy then appeared at warp speed from PE, running the length of the atrium and out onto the yard in his pants, yelling with laughter. Fully clothed mates followed behind.

I retrieved the lot of them and lined them up indoors. Establishing that it was a joke rather than abuse I gave them an old-fashioned response and sent them back into the changing rooms with fleas in their ears. Head of PE took it over from there.

Head of Year 7 tapped on my shoulder once I was done and whispered 'prospective parents, one's a journalist'. Sure enough, two visitors at the other end of the atrium had witnessed all. Rolling our eyes at each other, I went to face the music. 'What must you think of us? A boy in underwear and me yelling at them. It's not usually like this. In fact, it's never been like this.'

They laughed and said they'd enjoyed the clear guidance I'd offered, the sheepishness of the youths and the brisk addressing of the issue. They still moved house into the catchment area. It's not always like that, either.

It will be useful at this point to apply our four tests of professionalism to see whether, in this tangled knitting of relationships, we understand the best relationship of professionalism for parents through the tests of consent, constraint, expertise and benefit.

## Consent

Despite the picture I paint most parents are happy with their child's schooling and happy to work with the school. They understand, explicitly or tacitly, that the school will do its best. They want the dual functions of the school to be upheld equally well. They expect the English and maths grades to open the doors of prosperity in later life but they also entrust schools to share in the formation of the beloved child's character. They gladly **consent**, not to sharing parenting as that is not in their gift, but to support the school when it is *in loco parentis*.

That relationship is legally defined. The school's role as a parent is not a responsibility delegated by the home parent but given to the school by the state. Parents do not allow schools to look after their children; the state empowers and requires schools to do so. Bluntly, when a child is at school, the state-parent power of the school trumps that of the parents themselves. That's a big responsibility and it is a testament to the school leaders of the land that it is so consistently upheld.

## Constraint

The second test is of **constraint**, when the educational economies of scale I described earlier affect the relationship. The professional parenting we offer in school is a mixture of what we think is right, what we can prove to be useful, what the nation values and what we can afford. It is often constraint that causes the angry barge into reception: why can't my child have the special treatment she deserves? It is rare that this can't be resolved, but not unknown. Sometimes parents are so angry about education that they set themselves completely against the school, withholding any consent for anything. Sometimes the school has to carry on parenting within constraints and without consent.

Constraint is also present when parenting is dangerous to the child. Most schools devise some sort of partnership so that the child is thoroughly protected. School leaders are inclined to opine that 'all parents want the best for their children' but it's not as easy as that. What of the child whose parents are violent or neglectful, obsessed with money or status, disregarding of learning, racist or addicted? Most parents want what they think is best for their children, but some parents are toxic and the school needs to ameliorate their effect if the child is to grasp at any happiness, let alone success or prosperity. Relations may be constrained – but the child must come to school.

## Expertise

In both the above, the **expertise** of the professional is required. A good school enables parents to be partners in the upbringing of the child and welcomes them into school. There will be formal and informal structures – parent consultations, coffee mornings, quiz nights, PTFAs and governor elections. The school want the child to be settled, happy and able to learn. A worried or conflicted child cannot do any of those so the relationships with difficult parents need to be managed. It is rare that a school leader will make the decision that a parent will no longer be welcome in school, or that a child's needs require social care intervention. Those are the kinds of decisions that stop professionals sleeping, but the shared responsibility of *in loco parentis* means that hard judgements, however unpalatable, have to be made.

And it's worth remembering the expertise the parent appreciates. The curriculum expertise of the school means that their child can now learn maths as they never did and their pride can be wonderful to behold. Schools' pastoral expertise gives a parent someone to turn to who is less weepy and flappy than they are themselves; 'It's OK, teenagers are often like this' can be of huge comfort to strung-out parents.

## Benefit

Finally, what **benefit** accrues to the child from the professional working in role for and with parents? That is found in the aggregated effects of our journey so far. The parenting the child receives at home is likely to be warm and loving. The *in loco parentis* professional has his own version of this: a safe and orderly community led by kind and expert adults. The benefit is the wraparound example of the good life that the child witnesses and learns. This isn't about wealth or status, success or competition. It has nothing to do with the externals of schooling, with provision structures or management, but everything to with the virtues and values, the behaviour of the adults on both sides of the parenting divide. The child's greatest benefit from the professional working as and with parents is that she will learn how to be fully human.

## Paradigm parent

The school is entrusted to be not just a good parent but a paradigm parent to the child. How is it equipped to do that? Not just through its powers but the fulfilment of its role, its fulfilment of the expectations of the state about the care of the state's children. While society may see that in terms of the service those children will render the democracy as adults, that is not the sole role of the professional educator. As they serve the child in the moment and teach them how to live, they must model the best hopes for children. We expect that of all parents. Whether the state understands what that means is a matter for the next chapter.

# 6 The professional for the state

## What are schools for?

Someone has to do it so I went on a Teachers' International Professional Development visit to California, ostensibly to look at the use of IT so close to Silicon Valley. As it happened, the use of IT was substantially behind most schools in the UK: we were in the technology boomtime of Building Schools for the Future.

The learning for me was about the schools' roles in their communities. The locally supported football team was the school team; the band everyone went to hear was the school band. The boundaries between institution and small town were porous and supportive. There was no competition between schools but deep historic links and shared knowledge through the way teacher and leader deployment worked.

A different world, faulty in some aspects no doubt, but very attractive. The school's success was the community's success, and they worked hard to support one another. They had common cause in the good of the children.

If you were to ask this chapter's question of the traveller on the Clapham omnibus he would probably say something that added up to *schools keep children safe, teach them right from wrong, how to think and what will be useful when they have to earn their own living.* He might also have opinions on such things as exam results and good manners (and believe teachers to be either saints or slackers). Further than that, not much. Schools are part of life, a universal compulsory public service. Surely we know what they're for?

Returning to the school gate, our parent's view is of an actual public institution with a public presence, an actual building in a street and community that may be existentially encountered. These are funded by the state's investment of taxpayers' money and they don't come cheap. A school building may have cost as much as hundreds, even thousands of local houses, as much as a hospital, a town hall, a police station. The teachers in the building are paid more than the national average salary and a headteacher will be paid many times more. There'll be an annual budget turnover in millions, perhaps double figures of millions. A school is a considerable undertaking representing a considerable investment.

So the angry parent bursting through the door is also asking the institution a reasonable question on behalf of the taxpayer. It's rarely framed as 'What am I getting for my money?' but it is underpinned by the language of reasonable entitlement. It might hint at 'Given that this is a nice building, you're comparatively well paid, and your working conditions even with Year 9 on a Wednesday afternoon are way better than mine in the chicken factory, why haven't you done better by my child? What redress may I have for such misuse of public funds?'

Behind this lies the role of the professional working for, with and on behalf of the state. School leaders work for the state in that they are paid from the public purse; they work with the state when they fulfil their duties diligently; they work on behalf of the state when they realise the hopes and aims that the state has for education, on behalf of all its people. This is a reasonable extrapolation from the status quo, but it is insufficiently theorised or even explained. We talk about education in terms of learning and outputs, not the role it plays in civic society. Where to start?

## A safe place

The duty schools have to keep children safe is extensively covered as a result of panics, tragedies and legislation. Statutory documents such as Keeping Children Safe in Education give clear directions about the responsibility of the school, its staff and leadership, to fulfil the state's duty of care. There are instructions about protecting children, identifying neglect and abuse, where and how to report it, which senior post-holders should be appointed, how staff should be recruited and their past lives checked, how their work should be monitored by governors and board members, and the manner in which schools will be held to account by inspectors. Keeping children safe is everyone's concern; it is a social duty in which schools have a particularly important and central role to play. It is schools which act on behalf of the state to protect the nation's young. Our Clapham commuter should be satisfied by that.

In this statutory structure the buck stops with the head. If safeguarding is found to be faulty, or if a child is avoidably harmed, the consequences are severe. A school leader's tenure is at risk if such a thing happens, or is uncovered. There is a level of personal responsibility that is probably quite reasonable – though most actual heads would say that reporting a concern and a concern being resolved are two different issues.

Imagine the experience known to most schools, the Friday-afternoon-before-a-holiday disclosure. A child, frightened of home, facing the prospect of a weekend or, worse, weeks of abuse without the safety of the school, will come to a trusted adult. The referral is made, but other players are legitimately busy elsewhere: social services have huge caseloads, the police are responding to crime and danger. The clock ticks and the Designated Safeguarding Officer (DSO) and the head are still at school with a terrified child at six in the evening, or later. The school, on behalf of the state, has the child. What to do? She's got no one to trust outside school, she can't be turned out onto the street, the DSO can't take the child home, but the caretaker needs to lock up. County Hall has gone home and the duty officer is in the middle of something worse, so the child in extremis is given to the police, who will then look after her on behalf of the state until the next guardian may be found. The professionals act for the child, and for the state.

Is this what schools are for? Yes, but it is an underpinning duty and one relatively recently enjoined upon them. Schools have existed for centuries without much explicit attention being given to their safeguarding duty. In fact, some schools in some traditions have been actively harmful to schools but still survived into the modern and even postmodern era.

## Places of learning

The primary function of the school is to teach. Schools were set up from antiquity onwards, to pass on knowledge and ways of being that the setters-up valued enough to wish to preserve beyond the current generation. Schools' curricula supported the formation of the young: the Trivium in Ancient Rome; the classics and a little mathematics in the English public schools from the sixteenth century onwards. Practical skills in the post-war secondary moderns; the skills of the professional classes in the grammar schools.

The content and subjects of the curriculum represent something about society and what the state values. An educated person, we might think, knows a little of history and literature, can recognise a famous tune and name the bones of the skeleton. She can cope with a little algebra and exchange pleasantries or ask for help in a foreign language. He can put up a shelf, make a nutritious meal, appreciate a painting and the offside rule. She can keep fit, respect another's religion, calculate speed and understand why copper goes green. If he's lucky, there might be more. Eventually, he might make a choice as to which of these areas of knowledge he enjoys the most and seek to learn more deeply. Or she might find a congenial way of earning a living, reading novels at bedtime or playing for a team. He'll know why it's important to vote, to avoid sexually transmitted diseases, and tell the truth.

As to the subject content of the curriculum, we have spent many years at sea. English schools got a National Curriculum in 1988. The Education Act 2002 revised it so that maintained schools would provide 'a balanced and broadly based curriculum that:

- promotes the spiritual, moral, cultural, mental and physical development of learners at the school and within society and

- prepares learners at the school for the opportunities, responsibilities and experiences of adult life.'

(Education Act 2002, para 78, p53)

This curriculum framework sought to guarantee an entitlement for learners of all backgrounds to standards, continuity and coherence, and which would aid public understanding. It should instil in children a positive disposition to learning, and a commitment to learn and promote and pass on essential knowledge, skills and understanding valued by society to the next generation.

The National Curriculum was reviewed again in 2008. Reviewer Mick Waters set the tone:

> The curriculum should be treasured. There should be real pride in our curriculum; the learning that the nation has decided to set before its young. Teachers, parents, employers, the media and the public should all see the curriculum as something to embrace, support and celebrate. Most of all, young people should relish the opportunity for discovery and achievement that the curriculum offers.

This curriculum had *Values* at its heart:

> Education should reflect the enduring values that contribute to personal development and equality of opportunity for all, a healthy and just democracy, a productive economy, and sustainable development.

The National Curriculum was controversial from the start among existing school leaders. To many, it was an anodyne committee-devised series of unwieldy lists and performance indicators which immediately stripped schools and school leaders of one of their fundamental roles, to set up a good curriculum for their children, in that place. Martin Roberts has written eloquently about this.

> Like most of my colleagues I was initially shocked when I realised that the government were serious about implementing a National Curriculum. Such a policy attacked directly the culture of teacher control which my generation had taken for granted.
>
> (Roberts 2014: 125)

Nonetheless, to a headteacher of my generation, the National Curriculum was a given, on tablets of stone and weighing nearly as much. Curriculum design was what the timetabler did when they tried to fit the subjects the school valued into the timetable slots available, especially at Key Stage 4 when children had some choice about what to study to GCSE level.

Simultaneously, the development of public accountability measures for schools placed a pressure on curriculum design that eventually bent it out of shape. The universal SATs tests for 11-year-olds and the GCSE qualification for 16-year-olds became, with safeguarding, the measure of schools' effectiveness. The inspection provider Ofsted put its inspectors on the roads to assess schools according to these, and a changing list of lesser performance indicators. The rise of deliverance methodology in government and feverish political promises about '*education, education, education*' required public sector targets which could be used to demonstrate to the taxpayer that they were getting value for money. The role of the professional began to be compared to football managers, where heads were one bad Ofsted away from a P45.

But curriculum is one thing and accountability another. The flexibilities of the qualifications valid for the performance tables and the ways in which success was calculated sowed the wind and reaped the whirlwind. As Alison Wolf observed in her report:

> The perverse incentives created by performance measures . . . resulted in large amounts of sub-standard education, in which young people took courses that were in no sense truly 'vocational' or useful.
>
> (Wolf, cited in Stewart 2011)

A change of government in 2010, therefore, brought further review and the curriculum became fully conflated with examination and accountability. Secretary of State Michael Gove vowed:

> To replace the current substandard curriculum with one based on the best school systems in the world . . .

Aspects of this new curriculum would:

- embody rigour and high standards and create coherence

- ensure all children have the opportunity to acquire a core of essential knowledge in the key subject disciplines

- allow teachers the freedom to use their professionalism and expertise

- give teachers greater professional freedom over how they organise and teach the curriculum

- enable parents to understand what their children should be learning throughout their school career and therefore to support their education

(Gove 2011)

So, the state has specific aims for its children through the prime focus of schools on learning. And, the state expects parents to agree with its view on the content and purpose of the curriculum.

That this was restated and enforced in the teeth of the profession's opposition and terror is worth considering from an ethical perspective. The focus of the curriculum, rather than the learning of the child, had become their validation of schools through accountability measures of performance tables and inspection. Sadly, school leaders had been prepared to trade curriculum thinking for delivery. This led to teaching for the benefit of the school rather than the education of the child. As it happ ened at a time of deregulation and intense focus on the personal attributes of the leader, an ethical ambiguity attendant on combining curriculum, accountability and leadership remuneration became a factor in the state's system.

The inspection service was itself at a time of change. Russell Hobby, of the National Association of Head Teachers, expressed its predicament well.

> We stand at a turning point with Ofsted. The education system has been transformed since the inspectorate was created. The question now is whether Ofsted can keep pace . . . Ofsted needs the courage to look beyond raw data and ask how the results have been achieved. We cannot build sustainably good schools if leaders are always in fear of one bad year.
>
> (Hobby, cited in Weale 2016)

Or, as one might say, we cannot build sustainably good schools if the accountability measures turn good heads into bad or frightened people.

Amanda Spielman (HMCI from 2017) rightly criticised schools for tactics used to bolster performance-table standings. She cited examples of primary pupils sitting mock SAT tests for more than two years and secondary schools entering students for accountable qualifications requiring just two days of study to pass.

> This all reflects a tendency to mistake badges and stickers for learning itself. And it is putting the interests of schools ahead of the interests of the children in them. We should be ashamed that we have let such behaviour persist for so long.

Where society seeks to value a complex enterprise such as education using easily measurable outcomes as part of government-term targets, heads as public servants serve the public's will. If that means that the curriculum and its measures are dictated from above, then we comply. It is easy to criticise school leaders for mistaking proxies (examination assessment) for our goals (learning and knowledge), but that was what the state required. It did not require principled curriculum thinking from its headteachers – though many sought to preserve this. The problem was rooted firmly in a historically shallow understanding of the purpose of education. What are schools for?

It was in working with the curriculum thinker Michael F D Young that I had the chance to study and crystallise my own understanding of this purpose. His reassessment of his own views over time in *Bringing Knowledge Back In* (Young 2008) was quickly influential. It appealed to curriculum thinkers, and the 'neo-traditionalists' clustering around the Department for Education at the time. It repays careful reading so here's my own summary:

Teachers are the people who offer powerful knowledge to the nation's children. That knowledge comes from centuries of learning and from the universities and subject associations. It is powerful because it enables children to interpret and control the world. It is fair and just that this should be so. It is unfair and unjust when children are offered poor-quality knowledge which fails to lift them out of their experience.

This is a more subtle approach than the fevered debate of the time would allow. A tendency to hark back to a golden age of learning which has never existed in England usually leads to misapprehension of the presenting issue in schools. The Department's solution – to overhaul every aspect of every qualification and their calibration, and tighten accountability's grip on the curriculum still further – caused five more years of turbulence in schools.

Some justification for returning to, or devising, content-heavy curricula was attributed to the American educationalist E D Hirsch (1987), to whom was consistently misattributed a Gradgrindian preference for facts. Hirsch's project was cultural literacy: he wrote in the defence of poor, nomadic or non-WASP children for whom the differing federal curriculum content acted as a barrier to participation in national life. He challenged education's policy-makers to require US states to include the knowledge children needed to understand and therefore prosper within the dominant culture. His example list, loved by neo-traditionalists but loathed by UK school leaders of the early 2010s, is a practical guide to 'what literate Americans know'. It is a clear and useful example of the chasm between the word-rich and the word-poor into which children can fall. It is not a conservative view, but one from the left, arguing for social justice.

Hirsch's greater commitment, however, is to what he describes as the *The Common School and the Common Good* (1996: 235).

> Improving the effectiveness and fairness of education through enhancing both its contents and its commonality has a more than educational significance. The improvement would . . . diminish the educational iniquities with the nation. Nothing could be more important to our national wellbeing than overcoming these inequities . . . But something equally significant is at stake. Many observers have deplored the decline in civility in our public life and with it the decline in our sense of community. The inter-ethnic hostilities . . . the astonishing indifference to the condition of our children all bespeak a decline in the communitarian spirit. In the long run, that could be the common school's most important contribution to preserving the fragile fabric of our democracy.

Quite. This echoes the 1988 National Curriculum's aim to sustain democracy which, in its turn, gives an ethical foundation to guide school leaders and give children the best education. While politicians of all shades developed a taste from 1988 for tinkering with the curriculum, they have underplayed the role of schooling in the preservation of the common good. It is a re-examination of the purpose of schooling that is needed, not a rearrangement of its proxies

It would therefore be helpful if that purpose could be clearly agreed so that good teachers' and leaders' self-understanding might truly serve the state. Inspired by Young and Hirsch, I first worked up 10 points to help my own staff understand the complexity of their professional task. I use them frequently.

1  **Knowledge is worthwhile in itself.**

We should tell children this unapologetically and celebrate it in our schools: It's what childhood and adolescence is for

2  **Schools teach shared and powerful knowledge on behalf of society.**

We teach children what they need to make sense of and improve the world

3  **Shared and powerful knowledge is verified through learned communities.**

What we teach is accurate and current, and we act as model lifelong learners

4  **Children need powerful knowledge to understand and interpret the world.**

Without it they remain dependent upon those who have it or misuse it

5  **Powerful knowledge is cognitively superior to that needed for daily life.**

It transcends and liberates children from their daily experience

6  **Shared and powerful knowledge enables children to grow into useful citizens.**

As adults they can understand, cooperate and shape the world together

7  **Shared knowledge is a foundation for a just and sustainable democracy.**

Citizens educated together share an understanding of the common good

8  **It is fair and just that all children should have access to this knowledge.**

Powerful knowledge opens doors: it must be available to all children

9  **Accepted adult authority is required for shared knowledge transmission.**

The teacher's authority to transmit knowledge is given and valued by society.

10  **Pedagogy links adult authority, powerful knowledge and its transmission.**

Quality professionals enable children to make a relationship with ideas to change the world.

This places the taught curriculum in the context of the purpose of schooling. Ethically, its use confers legitimacy on sound curriculum development: curriculum not just as a tool, but a public good. Knowledge, engagement, good learning from well-qualified teachers, effective curriculum thinking and sensible timetabling in schools, a principled commitment to fair opportunities, a bold understanding of the common good, a commitment to quality teaching and the expectation that society will understand, value and support the enterprise. If we could share such a vision, such an understanding, we could liberate schools, their curricula and most importantly their children from the short-term priorities of the political cycle. As Cicero may have said:

'What greater and better gift can we offer the republic than to teach and to instruct our young?'

## The moral development of the child

My loquacious bus companion of the opening of this chapter assigned another responsibility to schools and their leaders, that of teaching children good manners, and its underpinning, good character.

I discussed in the previous chapter the expectation and understanding that schools – with or perhaps rather than parents – will also teach children how to behave and the norms of civilised society. Frequent panics that this might not be the case, from sex education to radicalisation, tend to add to the requirement of schools to pass on the prevailing morality and ethics of society. These are reflected in fluctuating lists in the Ofsted schedule for the perhaps unmeasurable inspection of 'social, moral spiritual and cultural development'. Despite this, there remains disagreement about the importance of such social mores, and the status of personal, social, cultural, health and relationships education is unclear. Should it be compulsory, for all schools?

In contrast, character education has recently been strongly encouraged in schools, also inserted into the inspection schedule. This deserves closer attention for two reasons. First, it coincides with the curriculum redevelopment which has radically increased the subject content of general qualifications. Second, and the link between these two points is not proved, it coincides with an exponential rise in the incidence of mental health problems in young people.

The muddy semi-debate on the ill-defined 'fundamental British values' has encouraged most schools to produce lists of values. These focus decades of work on character into something so snappy a child can remember it to tell a visiting inspector. Character education, therefore, might fulfil the taxpayer's wish that children are taught right from wrong. It could even serve as a national consensus on virtue. My school has its list, of kindness, fairness, honesty, respectfulness and optimism. Other schools have longer ones, often including the grit 'n' resilience attributed to the cadet corps of the public schools and currently enjoined upon the poor. We devise these lists in consultation with children, parents, governors, teachers. We think of subtle or crass ways of encouraging or enforcing them. We conduct assemblies on the absolute worth of such personal virtues. In order to name them for our children, we can pluck virtues valued by the good state seemingly from the air.

Headteachers have long said that such explicit values help young people become good citizens. Character is reinforced by classroom rules, school behaviour policies, and ancient mottoes and inspirational slogans proclaim assumed norms and goods: *Education through Excellence, Sapere Aude, Achievement through Care, Education to understand the world and change it for the better, Honore et labore, Not for Thyself Alone.* These range from personal virtues such as truthfulness and good temper through broad characteristics such as conscientiousness and trustworthiness to perhaps more contestable beliefs: conformity, diligence, obedience or compliance with authority and local regulations such as uniform and punctuality. Consequently, most schools are safe and orderly communities where large groups of children and young people behave in a cooperative and harmonious manner, a model of community cohesion that the adult citizenry would do well to mimic.

## Leading well: what do heads think and say?

So, children are encouraged to develop the personal virtues and behaviours that adults know will make them better citizens. It is reasonable to assume that this will be developed in their schools both through instruction and example. The headteacher is expected to be able to provide both. The needs of the child and the good state coalesce in her leadership of the model community but the fundamental underpinnings of this duty are underthought in our system. What are the ethics we teach and live?

School leaders are not entirely clueless on this matter. They largely run happy and safe communities and must get their inspiration from somewhere. Ask a group to identify ethical principles, even the Principles for Public Life (Nolan 1994) and they struggle, but their guesswork is pretty reliable: honesty, trustworthiness, transparency. When pressed they tend to shy away from first-order virtues and clutch onto products or outcomes such as leadership and integrity, or even adjectival abstractions like excellence. Part of the reason for this may be a very British embarrassment about claiming too much, appearing to take oneself too seriously or sounding religious. But the taxpayer on the Clapham omnibus expects us to have a secure moral compass and to demonstrate in our own behaviour that which we teach the children. The angry parent in reception expects to be greeted by a good person who will treat him kindly, fairly and consistently. He does not expect us to lie or to be greedy or fraudulent, to be prejudiced against him or his child. He does not expect his child to be seen purely as examination yield.

When, then, are school leaders to discuss the values and virtues of their own behaviour? If there is a reluctance this may worryingly be attributed to the current pressures on school leadership, where regulation and compliance play the dominant role. There is no room or time for discussion of anything which does not directly contribute to worse outcomes in the performance tables. This leads to a paralysing focus on compliance with external measures. School leaders are so frightened of losing their jobs that they cannot give time, even in their self-conceptualisation, to any idea for which there is no metric in the accountability measures or compliance tick-list to prove that a standard has been reached.

In this way, the intense pressure of high-stakes accountability exerts pressure on both parts of the school leader's role. In accordance with the wishes of the state he instils honesty and respect in his young people. The system, however, exerts an opposing pressure. In order to keep his school afloat, he may feel compelled to finesse the truth in his publicity and threaten colleagues with dismissal when impossible targets aren't met. Fearful for the future of his school, his professional reputation and his mortgage, he focuses on compliance and the metrics of accountability. What else should he do?

It is for this reason that we need to develop a shared language of ethics for school leaders. If we agree that certain characteristics, values and virtues are valuable to develop in children so that they become good citizens, then we must already have a view of the fundamental principles that make good citizens. If we can agree and explain them, then the risk of us ignoring, skewing or convening them is mitigated. If our schools were built on explicit, shared ethical foundations we could really set the best example to the nation's children.

## Personal and professional values

What might these be? In their private lives, adults largely know what we want for our own families and what makes for a good society. At home most of us try to model love, wit, honesty, good temper, magnanimity, reciprocity, duty, kindness, service, hope and all the virtues of a good life. Human frailty brings us down but neighbours help and support each other to survive and flourish. We know that wealth and status don't amount to strength of character and that kindness is more important than dominance. Right ambition is – well – right, and more praiseworthy than the other kind. Could we agree that such values and virtues are central to our public endeavour? Could we agree a set of ethical principles for our work on behalf of the state?

Is it helpful to start with private virtues and see if we can apply them to our professional role? Let us look at some basic examples of ethics in practice.

> A leader might be able to run a school well despite an occasional error of judgement. This could be a poor-quality appointment, or a temporarily overheated budget, or an honest error in exam entries. If he stays on the right end of a continuum from mistakes through incompetence to lies, resolves problems quickly and his school runs reasonably successfully, he should be safe to practice.

But what about these?

- Should you run a school if you are unfaithful to your partner and lie about it?
- Should you run a school if you have been banned from driving because of drinking?
- Should you run a school if you have a conviction for domestic violence?
- Should you run a school if you deliberately submit fraudulent tax returns?

We might produce answers such as:

- Yes. Society accepts some dissonance in matters of love.

- Yes, if it was a single error of judgement but not if you're an unreformed alcoholic because that will consistently impair your judgement and make you an unsafe state parent: you lack temperance.

- No, because it's a crime, and it demonstrates cruelty, which always damages others, especially children. You lack self-control, which is important to develop in young people.

- No, because it's a crime and you need to be trusted with public money. You are dishonest and untrustworthy. You lack truthfulness.

All of the above are hard to deal with. They are embarrassing to the adults involved and provide dangerous role models for the nation's young. The second pair might require whistleblowing at the very least. But what about activities internal to the school?

- Should you run a school if your behaviour towards staff makes them so fearful they can't function properly?

- Should you run a school if you encourage or turn a blind eye to malpractice?

- Should you run a school if you are prepared to off-roll difficult children to improve your outcome scores?

- Should you run a school if you set up legal companies so you and your family may be paid more from school budget than your salary indicates?

- Should you run a school if you want to be paid a salary way beyond the conventions of the system?

The answer to each of the above is 'no'. Discovering any of these actions should make a leader's position untenable both as a public servant and a role model. These actions demonstrate the absence of good temper, humility, trust, kindness, truthfulness, prudence, honesty, selflessness, conscientiousness, service, accountability and openness. These are virtues that adults recognise and value in their personal lives. However, some of the above are current within our system and successful leaders (as judged by the system's internal calibrations) might be tempted by them. It might help us all if we had a language to tackle such things.

It is a short step from this to looking at actual examples of professional misconduct. In just three days in August 2017 the following stories appeared in the press.

1   A front-page article in the *Sunday Times* on academy heads' pay especially criticising those heads paid more than the Prime Minister. This was followed immediately by a piece on *BBC London News* about pay in a particular academy chain.

2    A front-page article in the *Guardian* on the proclivity of a noted grammar school to remove children from its roll at the end of Year 12 if their examination results meant they were unlikely to get A* – B at A level.

3    A widely shared report on senior staff at two ancient public schools being investigated for examination malpractice, in telling students what was going to appear on Pre-U papers.

Let schools without sin cast the first stones. All teachers and school leaders can negotiate our salaries: that's the basis of performance-related pay. All have worried over the effects of underachieving children on performance tables. All have had to dismiss teachers for malpractice.

## What would be an ethical response?

1    At a time of reduced spending on schools it is wrong for one person to be paid as much as 10 teachers. The children's needs are best met by having more teachers.

2    All universities do not require A* – B grades. A C – E grade as a result of honest endeavour is a valuable outcome. The value of the child's work is not the same as the A level performance table, which is only important to the school. The child's needs must come first and the distant, abstract argument that the needs of more children over time are met by the success of a school is erroneous. Present children cannot be sacrificed to the needs of future children.

3    The purpose of an examination is to test knowledge fairly and objectively. If an examiner leaks the question to some children, the whole structure is undermined. Those entrusted to keep a confidence should do so.

We can go further and use these examples of national outrage as a way of extrapolating moral principles.

1    It is wrong to use public money egregiously to enrich oneself.

2    Each child's endeavour should be valued equally.

3    It is wrong to cheat.

Schools generally have this covered. We tell it to children from the tinies on the mat to the 18-year-olds who don't fit onto assembly chairs:

1    Don't steal.

2    Treat everyone equally.

3    Always be trustworthy.

You can try this method for yourself. There are stories about school leadership readily available in the press, monthly if not weekly – though some may be egregious misrepresentations.

## So, what should we do?

We know the social values we want to protect into the next generation. Our problem may be believing them enough to keep them ourselves, in the decisions we make as school leaders, as professionals working with, for and as the state.

We worry we can't live up to human ethical standards in our professional lives so we find ourselves in a terrific pickle. We know our system has to be regulated and monitored, but we have grown so fearful of the destructive potential of regulation on our schools and careers that we have embraced compliance like drowning people. We don't want to be professionally held to the wider values of a good society because our structures sometimes prevent us from reaching them. If I'm honest about my results the school might close. If I put a child's mental health before his exam results I'm 'an enemy of promise' (Gove 2013).

It's not that we don't know what's right or wrong. We are familiar with compromise and ambiguity. We understand, sadly, that people with the right intentions may feel trapped into bad behaviour to secure their schools or their jobs. Our real fear should be that our system doesn't know or care if school leaders are good or bad as long as schools meet targets. This paralyses leaders who fear failure, insecurity and humiliation. Subsequently, we turn our back on the dreadful example such timidity and box-ticking sets the young and hope that someone, somewhere is showing them a better way to live.

But schools are where society looks after its young until they are old enough to assume the mantle of adult citizenship. All school performance indicators are proxies for the good society, sufficient but not necessary. Schools may rail against accountability measures, but few still argue – as they did in the 90s – that accountability is impertinent and undermines a profession. Good schools, however, need more than targets and compliance mechanisms. Their work should be rooted in the virtues we value most and which we would want everyone everywhere to espouse as a way of life. When we've courageously and publicly decided what they are, we must demonstrate them in ourselves before we teach them to our young.

## Testing professional headship

It is time then to turn our attention to the four tests of professionalism we have discussed in the preceding chapters. How do school leaders demonstrate consent, constraint, expertise and benefit through their work as professionals for the state?

### Consent

School leaders work as professionals on behalf of the state with the state's consent. That consent is given for, arguably, the most important work the state can do, the formation of the young. School leaders are drawn from the ranks of teachers, whose subject or pedagogical expertise is assessed and authorised by the state.

That consent is given in the understanding that schools will instil a love of learning in their pupils. That is realised and validated through the curriculum and its outcomes. Consent is also given in the understanding that schools will instil an understanding of right and wrong in their pupils. That is realised and validated by their behaviour as they grow, and as adult citizens in the future. The taxpayer can scrutinise the actions of the school in generating learning though their children's outcomes, which is linked to the quality of teaching provided by the leader. It is harder to scrutinise the actions of a school in generating good character. Society has to be able to trust the good character, intentions and actions of those setting an example of adult conduct to the young. That is why the ethics of school leadership are so crucial to the contract we have with the taxpayer.

## Constraint

The constraints of this relationship are to do with the structures which regulate the roles, purposes and interactions of adults and children in schools. Five issues currently – perhaps usually – present themselves to school leaders:

- Funding: how can we meet the state's expectations with the funding available?

- Curriculum: what and how should we teach?

- Teachers: why is teaching so unattractive as a career? What can we do about it?

- Accountability: what is being measured and how reliably? What impact should this have on the previous decisions?

- Leadership: given all of the above, who'd be a headteacher?

Constraint, however, should not undermine the faith which the state reasonably invests in us when it consents to our partnership. It is not acceptable to abdicate responsibility. It undermines the professional contract if school leaders say:

> A regulator wants 90% of children to do a certain set of subjects by 2025 so I will plan to achieve that whether I think it right or wrong educationally. I can strain every sinew to reach a progress score of 0 and when I have done both, then I will have a good school. Whatever the regulators want is the total good for the system.

We have to be able to balance our responsibility as professionals with our responsibility as public servants. As professionals we are expected to share in developing accountability, not to be its passive and frantic recipients. In order to do that, we need to have faith in our own judgements and a shared language in which to express them from first principles.

## Expertise

It follows that we will take a view on the way in which education should be structured and schools run. If schools are where society looks after its young, then the professionals leading them should be concerned with how well we are doing it. Again, it is not acceptable to abdicate responsibility, or just to wait for instruction.

For example, school leaders share an increasing concern that the mechanisms and processes of schools, the tensions between measurable outputs of a functionalist curriculum and the welfare of the child, might be causing them actual harm. Our experience and expertise require us to propose a different way of working so that the metrics of accountability as experienced in our schools don't drive actual children to despair.

## Benefit

If one of the functions of the state is to develop through its law and institutions the habits of the good citizen, then schools are central to its success. If schools are run by a professional cadre of educators with a certain amount of freedom, then we invest huge hope in those people to identify and institutionalise the habits valued by the state. It's not too much to assert that schools are the proving ground for the state, test-beds for civic friendship, model societies in which the future civic health of the nation is assured. Their graduates could almost be hallmarked, stamped like the British lion that guarantees the health of our eggs.

The consent, constraint, expertise and benefits tied together in school leaders' professional relationship to the state are found in the parallel tracks of our responsibility. We have to be able and ready to reclaim our professional purpose in what we offer through our curricula and how we generate good conduct through teaching and example.

It is possible to make thoughtful professional judgements about what is good and bad for the state's children even if it's also hard to do. It is possible to decide, collectively, on right and wrong and be certain that some activities are good, some acceptable, and others insupportable. Developing a shared language of ethical leadership may be the best foundation for a healthy and successful relationship between the leader, the state and the child.

# Part 2
## Ethics and schools

# 7 Ethical thinking

I've always been fond of school councils, of the student voice. They tend to have obsessions with toilets, meals and uniform but that's because those are pretty fundamental to life. Careful manoeuvring can get them to talk seriously and fairly about curriculum and teaching styles but the whims of youth aren't far from the surface. Working with a mixed bunch of Year 7 and 8s to make life in a cold and dilapidated building bearable, I sent them out to canvass their peers. What would really make life better? Name it?

I imagined that 'being allowed to stay in at break' might rank highly, or 'places to sit on the yard', but no. What they all really agreed they wanted was bacon sandwiches and pony rides. Where to start? We held a seminar on animal welfare and decided that making ponies come to school as well would just be cruel. The bacon sandwiches took a year, but they happened, and went whole school when we moved. It was a lesson in getting things done, a little bit of training in changing the community

Eglantyne Jebb founded the Save the Children Fund in 1919. She said that it '. . . must not be content to save children from the hardships of life – it must abolish these hardships; nor think it suffices to save them from immediate menace – it must place in their hands the means of saving themselves and so of saving the world.'

Bacon sandwiches and pony rides are a start. Changing the world follows.

So far I have explored some complexities of school leadership and the context in which decisions – some clear, some of unavoidable ambiguity – have to be made. In subsequent chapters I will look at the kind of decisions school leaders face, and how they might go about making the right decisions to tackle them. This chapter gives an overview of different sorts of ethical thinking.

I take it for granted that there is a tension at the heart of this discussion. In most cases, a headteacher is expected to be able to make the right judgement and deal with whatever consequences arise. Schools are made up of a variety of human beings: children and adults. Sometimes problems are familiar and wisdom and experience lead quickly to a clear solution. Some problems, however, lurch from the complex to the dangerous and school leaders need to carefully consider the implications of their decisions. As captain of the ship, it is not always easy to ask for help.

I will start by providing a theoretical and practical structure for personal, institutional and system-wide ethical decision-making. Later on, we'll look at some worked examples which I hope are helpful, even diverting.

## Mapping the territory

In the UK everyone is educated to secondary level and this universal service provided by society, free at the point of delivery or bought from a commercial or charitable provider, works with the learning, personal and social development of young people from childhood to their lives as independent adults. Schools and colleges are the focus of the very highest hopes of young people, their families and wider society. Every child in the UK engages with the school system. Our ethics must place their needs at the heart of our decisions. Headteachers have highly complex professional duties and the ethical decisions they make (to do the right thing, achieve a good result) are of enormous significance to the development of society and individuals.

## Schools are organisations

Schools and colleges are complex organisations. They have similar powers and duties to other bodies which employ people, and work with the vulnerable. There are buildings and money for which governors and leaders have responsibility. Schools and colleges are often part of networks providing support, resources, direction and scrutiny: Local Authorities, Diocesan Boards of Education, and Academy structures. This guidance, cooperation and line management also need agreed common values.

## Schools share and make knowledge

When young people make the transition from school to adult life, the passport they carry needs to have a reliable basis in objective assessment. Schools and colleges play their part in giving young people access to, and the knowledge and learning to achieve in, each area of human civilisation. Integrity in intellectual and pedagogic life is the heart of professional teaching. Maintaining that sound independent assessment is the gold standard of qualifications.

## Schools are in the public domain

Apart from the complicated and precise agreed links between schools and the other agencies with whom a headteacher must work, schools are also subject to public debate. School leaders are bombarded with all sorts of advice and criticism. Everyone has been through school and uses the experience to plan, criticise or bury schools and their leaders.

Clearly structured ethical thought and decision-making also help heads know what to say in public. They have to speak for their school. They are also likely to be one of the few professional willing and able to interpret what children and young people are like and up to in a community.

The boundaries between education and employment require spirited and subtle defences of the practices, learning and qualifications of the school system. Everyone has an investment, everyone a view. How, then, should we act? Are there objective ways to make complex decisions?

## Ethical frameworks for school leaders

Ethicists use different approaches to judge right and wrong. Understanding them is central to structured ethical thought and sensible action. I will consider four approaches.

1   **Rights**: human rights are at the heart of our thinking. They are a powerful tradition with a particular importance to those who work with vulnerable people (and who is more vulnerable than a child?). Eglantine Jebb began claiming rights for children and young people through her refugee work after the First World War. The *United Nations Convention on the Rights of the Child* sums up current thinking and is expressed in national and European legislation.

2   **Duties:** how we should behave towards others is a strong tradition of ethical discussion from religion to Immanuel Kant and John Rawls. School leaders frequently find themselves stuck between Kant's insistence on always doing the right thing for each individual and John Stuart Mill's utilitarian approach benefiting the largest number of people. How do we justify our actions in community?

3   **Virtues:** Aristotle's Ethics invite us to consider what sort of people we want to be.

4   **Cases:** The centrality of cases in English common law demonstrates the value of the particular in making better judgements next time.

## Rights

A rights-based approach to ethics tries explicitly to codify areas of life that need protection. Naming specific activities from which children and young people should benefit (education) or defining society's resistance to specific risks (violence) reflect examples of bad behaviour at the individual or social level. Rights reflect times when the world has said 'never again' and set them up as barriers to resist future extreme abuses – even genocides.

For example, since 1997 the French government undertook a project to record on the outside of schools in Paris the precise numbers of pupils on roll in 1939–1944 who were taken to extermination camps. The wording describes how the children were taken:

> with the complicity of the government, under the period of Nazi barbarism, because they were born Jewish.
>
> (alamemoireparis.com)

Plaques recording these details now accompany the threefold slogan of the Republic and the school sign on the street. In these specific geographic contexts, rights cause pause for thought, in even the most amiable neighbourhoods.

Let's look at two codes of international rights that apply to our work.

The **United Nations Universal Declaration of Human Rights** was adopted by the General Assembly of the United Nations on 10 December 1948. **Article 26:1** sets out the universal right to education. **Article 26:2** begins:

> Education shall be directed to the full development of the human personality and to the strengthening of respect for human rights and fundamental freedoms.

I base what I say at my school on this: 'Education to understand the world, and change it for the better.'

## The United Nations Convention on the Rights of the Child

The origins of the UNCRC predate the UN's Universal Declaration of Human Rights and deserves our close attention. Eglantine Jebb drafted it through her *International Save the Children Union* for the League of Nations in 1924, following her work in Macedonia for the *Fight the Famine Council* which helped children starving as a result of the post-war Allied blockade of eastern Europe.

She said :

> I believe we should claim certain rights for the children and labour for their universal recognition, so that everybody – not merely the small number of people who are in a position to contribute to relief funds, but everybody who in any way comes into contact with children, that is to say the vast majority of mankind – may be in a position to help forward the movement.

This 1924 document had these five points.

1    The child must be given the means requisite for its normal development, both materially and spiritually.

2    The child that is hungry must be fed, the child that is sick must be nursed, the child that is backward must be helped, the delinquent child must be reclaimed and the orphan and the waif must be sheltered and succoured.

3    The child must be the first to receive aid in times of distress.

4    The child must be put in a position to earn a livelihood and must be protected against any form of exploitation.

5    The child must be brought up in the consciousness that its talents must be devoted to the service of its fellow men.

Expanded in 1948, the UN adopted a *Declaration of the Rights of the Child* with 10 principles in 1959, followed by the *Convention on the Rights of the Child* in 1989: 41 Articles defining the rights of children reflected in the laws of the signatory 'states parties'. Childhood is defined in 1989 as including everyone from birth to 18 years old.

In most countries, the school is where children and the state encounter each other. It is likely that teachers and school will be the first to know if a child's rights are being neglected. The school leader, therefore, has significant responsibility to ensure that the child's individual rights are protected in the way that the state wishes.

**Article 3** specifically requires that:

In all actions concerning children, whether undertaken by public or private social welfare institutions, courts of law, administrative authorities or legislative bodies, the best interests of the child shall be a primary consideration.

Some of the rights relate to school life, though they are framed about the whole of life.

**Article 12** defines children's rights to express their view about their life.

**Article 13** defines freedom of expression, particularly in terms of creative ideas and sharing information and ideas with others.

**Article 14** defends freedom of thought, conscience and religion.

**Article 15** defends freedom of association and peaceful assembly.

**Article 17** defends access to a wide range of media.

**Article 31** defends access to play and the arts.

All these apply to all young people. Other articles manage the boundaries of the school community preventing discrimination and exclusion, of:

**Article 23** those who are disabled.

**Article 27** those in poverty.

**Article 30** those from ethnic, religious or linguistic minorities.

Many of the articles directly address areas of children's lives where their age vulnerability makes them particularly susceptible to abuse by adults, either in their social setting or personal lives. For instance:

**Article 6** the right to life.

**Article 8** the right to a clear legal identity.

**Article 11** forbidding illicit transfer abroad.

**Article 19** protecting children from violence, injury or abuse.

**Article 20** special attention for children in care.

**Article 21** protection during adoption.

**Article 22** protection for refugees.

**Article 24** good quality nutrition and health.

**Article 26** covering child benefit.

**Article 27** the right to basic living standards.

**Article 32** protection from exploitation through work.

**Article 33** protection from drug abuse.

**Article 34** protection from sexual abuse.

**Article 35** protection from trafficking.

**Article 36** protection from all other abuse.

**Article 37** protection from torture.

**Article 38** protection from armed conflict and a ban on child soldiers

**Article 39** a commitment to rehabilitate children after any of the above.

**Articles 28 and 29** specifically concern education.

**Article 28**

1   States Parties recognize the right of the child to education, and with a view to achieving this right progressively and on the basis of equal opportunity, they shall, in particular:

    a   Make primary education compulsory and available free to all;

    b   Encourage the development of different forms of secondary education, including general and vocational education, make them available and accessible to every child, and take appropriate measures such as the introduction of free education and offering financial assistance in case of need;

    c   Make higher education accessible to all on the basis of capacity by every appropriate means;

    d   Make educational and vocational information and guidance available and accessible to all children;

e    Take measures to encourage regular attendance at schools and the reduction of drop-out rates.

2    States Parties shall take all appropriate measures to ensure that school discipline is administered in a manner consistent with the child's human dignity and in conformity with the present Convention.

3    States Parties shall promote and encourage international cooperation in matters relating to education, in particular with a view to contributing to the elimination of ignorance and illiteracy throughout the world and facilitating access to scientific and technical knowledge and modern teaching methods. In this regard, particular account shall be taken of the needs of developing countries.

**Article 29**

1    States Parties agree that the education of the child shall be directed to:

a    The development of the child's personality, talents and mental and physical abilities to their fullest potential;

b    The development of respect for human rights and fundamental freedoms, and for the principles enshrined in the Charter of the United Nations;

c    The development of respect for the child's parents, his or her own cultural identity, language and values, for the national values of the country in which the child is living, the country from which he or she may originate, and for civilizations different from his or her own;

d    The preparation of the child for responsible life in a free society, in the spirit of understanding, peace, tolerance, equality of sexes, and friendship among all peoples, ethnic, national and religious groups and persons of indigenous origin;

e    The development of respect for the natural environment.

2    No part of the present article or Article 28 shall be construed so as to interfere with the liberty of individuals and bodies to establish and direct educational institutions, subject always to the observance of the principle set forth in paragraph 1 of the present article and to the requirements that the education given in such institutions shall conform to such minimum standards as may be laid down by the State.

Human rights, whether interpreted as protection of children's interests or their freedom, exemplify yet another tension at the heart of school leaders' decision-making. As a citizen and *in loco parentis* heads must protect the humanity of the child, but also his freedom. They must do their best for them as vulnerably inexperienced human beings while they exercise their freedoms and grow into adult citizens. Every single decision made has to do both of those, according to the age of the child.

## Duties

Rights are the easy part of ethical leadership. They are enshrined in law and pretty simple to institutionalise in schools. Generally speaking, to an educated citizen of a liberal democracy, they don't present a problem. We wish these rights for ourselves; therefore we uphold them for our children.

Duties are closer to the heart and start to encroach upon the motivations we have for our actions. Remember, it is my contention that these motivations and actions should be dually scrutinised: how am I teaching the children in my school about the duties of interdependent humanity, and how am I modelling them myself? What decisions am I making, and how am I making them?

The German philosopher Immanuel Kant, arguably the founder of modern ethical thought, puts it pretty clearly. Adults have duties too because of the fundamental fact that children do not choose to be born. Therefore, making children's lives bearable is a consequence of the adult act of procreation (Metaphysics of Morals section 28) (Kant 1996:64).

If this isn't clear enough, we can apply it by analogy to school life. School staff are *in loco parentis* and children do not choose to be there. School leaders therefore have a duty to make children's lives as bearable as possible by running effective and humane schools. 'What would the good parent want?' is the starting point for uncovering duty in school.

Kant develops the Christian 'golden rule' from Matthew's gospel:

> In everything do to others as you would have them do to you (Matthew 7:12).

as his *categorical imperative*.

> Act only in accordance with that maxim through which you can at the same time will that it become a universal law.
>     (*Groundwork of the Metaphysics of Morals* 4:421; Kant 1997:31)

This *categorical imperative* is fundamental to any conception of the duties of service. School leaders should act in their schools and in their professional capacity as if their every action were to be universalised. How would it be if every school excluded children this way? Could the system afford for everyone to be paid like this?

John Rawls (1971) developed Kant's approach when he scrutinised progress towards the elusive equality promised by the American constitution. He argued that it is our duty to pursue *justice as fairness*. Justice is not worthy of the name if it does not improve the conditions of the most vulnerable, of those who have the most difficult lives. Equal opportunities are not enough because the advantaged remain advantaged: meritocracy can give the already-advantaged an easier swim to the top. Simply put, this is at the root of most government intervention designed to narrow gaps between disadvantaged and advantaged children.

So what to do? Rawls posited the *veil of ignorance* (1971:136). This veil means that when you make decisions about society, you don't know anything about your own position and attributes in that society. Social arrangements should work for everyone because they should reinforce a fair chance due to everyone. Social arrangements should work fairly no matter what the characteristics of the citizen, or his place in society, her assets, how intelligent he appears to be, even what she thinks is good. We should check that arrangements are fair by personal reflection: would it work fairly for me, or does it only work if I'm a healthy rich white male graduate? Simply put, it's why we remove identifying data from applications in fair recruitment processes.

Rawls wants to balance the demands of justice with those of freedom. This is not only important at a national level, but crucial in schools full of adolescents where they are growing from dependent childhood to independent lives as adults. Like rights, Rawls' proposals inform our desire to achieve both fairness and growing freedom for our young people while we protect them from others, and, for a while, from themselves.

So, his two *principles of justice* are:

1   The *Principle of Equal Liberty*

    Each person has an equal right to the most extensive liberties compatible with similar liberties for all.

2   The *Difference Principle*

    Social and economic inequalities should be arranged so that they are both

    a   To the greatest benefit of the least advantaged persons, and

    b   attached to offices and positions open to all under conditions of fair equality of opportunity.

Rawls recommends fine-tuning by applying the following rules:

1   Liberty may only be restricted to improve liberty for more people. One person's liberty may be constrained if more benefit. A restriction of liberty must be acceptable to those who have lesser liberty.

2   Justice is more important than efficiency or the greatest good for the greatest number. Fair opportunity is more important than difference. If inequality of opportunity is created it must help those with the least opportunity. For example, reducing a budget deficit must not unfairly affect those in the most hardship. High pay for a few managers must directly improve the lives of the most vulnerable.

Rawls both speaks to and challenges school leaders. We want to be fair, but some aspects of our education system privilege the advantaged over the disadvantaged. It could be argued that the existence of private schools disadvantages the most vulnerable and entrenches advantage. The practice of setting by ability, common in UK secondary schools, only advantages the most able: mixed-ability teaching raises standards more fairly. Building specific provision for and spending time and money on the most able through grammar schools disproportionately advantages those who are already winners in the lottery of life, but not to do so is castigated as lowering expectations. What is the greatest good for the greatest number? What would the good parent choose? What should the ethical leader do?

## Virtues

Finally, Aristotle (2000). Virtues are the personal characteristics of the leader that inform right judgement and decision-making. Aristotle's virtues set a new standard for systematic analysis of ethical thought in the fourth century BC. His approach can help analyse our options and actions as leaders, despite our distance from the time of Alexander the Great. His arguments in favour of each true virtue discern the right path by highlighting extremes to be avoided on either side. The following is his list, glossed by me.

1  **Courage** is about managing fear and confidence. We should act for the right even if we are frightened or physically threatened.

2  **Temperance** is about dealing with bodily pleasure and pain. We should respond well to physical pleasure, avoiding excess and asceticism.

3  **Generosity** is found in giving and receiving. We should avoid both wastefulness and stinginess.

4  **Magnificence** is found in using money on a large scale. We should spend well on important (even symbolic) matters, not being miserly, or ostentatiously spending the wrong way on the wrong things.

5  **Greatness of soul** is described as 'honour on a large scale'. We should have the capacity to take on a great honour, being neither vain nor 'small-souled' (overwhelmed).

6  **Even temper** means managing anger. We should be angry about the right things in the right way. A person who is always angry is irascible, a person who doesn't get angry when they should is foolish or oblivious.

7  **Friendliness** is found in social relations with large groups. We should be even-tempered with a wide range of people, not showing weakness in belligerence, or being only able to engage with a few types of people.

8  **Truthfulness** involves honesty about oneself. If we are boastful we exaggerate our skills but others are so self-deprecating they deny their capacity even for simple things.

9  **Wit** is conversational skill. We should avoid buffoonery or making a joke of everything as well as boorish, dull, dependent conversation. Wit's real virtue is to help conversation flow.

10 **Justice** is distributing things fairly. We should avoid both corruption and lawlessness.

11 **Friendship** is about dealing with individuals. We should seek to benefit the friend, not just seek personal pleasure or gain.

Aristotle's virtues go to the heart of the human experience. They seek to explain how a good person should behave and, allied to the virtues distilled into the 21st century from the ancient religions, give us a foundation for how to behave.

## Cases

Making judgements which consider all the above but are reinforced by the consistent reflective practice of studying cases is particularly important in England. Our legal tradition has no formal codification, so judges apply statutes and precedents from previous cases. The development of law is simultaneously clear and hidden, written and unwritten, immutable and changeable where previous decisions bind similar future cases.

Experienced school leaders rely on a sort of professional case law, using their wisdom, knowledge, understanding of the context and advice from other colleagues to make decisions. However, the *ad hoc*, individually driven and essentially private nature of this decision-making means that particular or peculiar practices may grow up unchecked. High-stakes accountability measures have been particularly susceptible to this: for example, the widespread use of GCSE-equivalent qualifications, for league-table purposes, which led to the curriculum reforms from 2011, grew by word of mouth which then segued into 'best practice'.

Adopting the formal processes of case law through the established mechanisms of the Public Inquiry and the general confidentiality of the Chatham House Rule could offer real learning for school leaders and benefit to schools. It could protect children as well as the leaders themselves and bring the profession into high repute. My practical proposal for this is in Chapter 16.

So, armed with four ways of looking at problems, how best is the school leader to act?

# 8 Ethics in public life

Years ago as a new head at the turn of the century, I accepted an invitation to an awards dinner at which my school was one of many also-rans. I sat next to an experienced head who uncovered my naivety pretty quickly and committed the rest of the evening to my development. When I next applied for a job, he said, I should know exactly what I wanted: a six-figure salary with bonuses, a decent car, private health care, gym membership, holidays in term time and so on. When I said that I didn't think that my governors would have been up for that sort of thing, he upbraided me not only for selling myself short but for letting down all heads everywhere. We deserve these things, and it's time we had them.

I couldn't be bothered to tell him that I strongly disapproved of everything he'd described as valuable, for a range of political, religious, professional and environmental reasons as well as an aversion to pointless exercise. I could have been braver and said 'it's wrong to spend taxpayers' money on toys and fripperies' but he would have said 'But we're worth it. Look at the job we do. Look at the bankers. Who's more important?'

## The 'Nolan Principles': Principles for Public Life

The year 1994 saw the founding of the Committee for Standards in Public Life. Not in itself an agency of measurement or accountability, it was designed to deter, prevent and respond to the kind of behaviour that brings down a government in the UK: corruption, nepotism, fraud, lies and a general untrustworthiness referred to at the time as 'sleaze'. The Nolan Principles (1994) and the supporting structure were set up by John Major's government in 1995 and their reach expanded to all public office holders under the Blair government.

Michael Nolan was put in charge of this development, which is why these seven Principles are often simply known as the 'Nolan Principles'. I set them out in their entirety below.

1  **Selflessness**: Holders of public office should act solely in terms of the public interest.

2  **Integrity**: Holders of public office must avoid placing themselves under any obligation to people or organisations that might try inappropriately to influence them in their work. They should not act or take decisions in order to gain financial or other material benefits for themselves, their family, or their friends. They must declare and resolve any interests and relationships.

3  **Objectivity**: Holders of public office must act and take decisions impartially, fairly and on merit, using the best evidence and without discrimination or bias.

4  **Accountability**: Holders of public office are accountable to the public for their decisions and actions and must submit themselves to the scrutiny necessary to ensure this.

5  **Openness**: Holders of public office should act and take decisions in an open and transparent manner. Information should not be withheld from the public unless there are clear and lawful reasons for so doing.

6  **Honesty**: Holders of public office should be truthful.

7  **Leadership**: Holders of public office should exhibit these principles in their own behaviour. They should actively promote and robustly support the principles and be willing to challenge poor behaviour wherever it occurs.

Insofar as we have a British standard for leading public institutions, these Principles constitute this. The Principles are clear and stately, almost to the point of stating the obvious. They appear to fall into two categories, relating to the public post and the public post-holder. One the one hand, the public post requires leadership, accountability and objectivity: on the other, these are based on the post-holder's personal qualities of selflessness, openness and honesty. The remaining principle, integrity, requires a post-holder to be undividedly good, with no awkward dissonance between the work-self and the personal-self. A gentlemanly person, one might once have perhaps said, whose responses are predictably wise, without a skeleton in any closet.

In that we can identify the dual role of the headteacher similarly, as the work-self (the public servant) and the personal-self (the exemplar), the Principles are a good starting point for us. How then might we use them to help protect and promote ethical behaviour in schools, and without them, what happens? We return to them later in a further refinement, but it may be useful now to experiment with their utility for school leaders and schools. After that, we depart on a brief excursion into why they seem so hard to achieve.

Mapping the attributes of the head to the Principles is straightforward.

- A **selfless** headteacher knows that she is passing through. He builds on the past strengths and works for the long term so that the next head takes on a seaworthy ship.

- A headteacher with **integrity** does the right thing even when no one is watching.

- An **objective** headteacher deals with everyone fairly, having no favourites or victims. She never bullies. Decisions are made on merit and with evidence.

- An **accountable** headteacher is willing and ready to be questioned by all stakeholders.

- An **open** headteacher is available, welcoming and friendly. She doesn't hide behind structures which dehumanise workplace relationships.

- An **honest** headteacher always tells the truth.

- Such a **leader** will tackle difficult issues as readily as easy ones and will be an absolutely reliable and predictable focus of unity for the school.

### *Let's develop our exploration.*

1   School leaders should be **selfless** and act only in the interest of children.

   A selfless school is part of a broad education system in which every child must be served. Every action should be designed to bring the benefits of education to all of a school's and a community's children. Therefore:

   a   All considerations of salary and status should be checked against this. It is wrong to divert money into excessive salaries if the children will benefit more from alternative expenditure, such as more teachers.

   b   The interest of children is the interests of *all* children, not only those in one school. So, for example 'off-rolling' children (taking steps to remove a child from the school roll other than by permanent exclusion) in order to improve accountability measures is wrong.

2   **Integrity.** School leaders must avoid placing themselves under any obligation to people or organisations that might try inappropriately to influence them in their work. They should not act or take decisions in order to gain financial or other material benefits for themselves, their family or their friends. They must declare and resolve any interests and relationships. Further, a school with integrity will deal with its public assets according to the strictest audit principles.

Therefore:

a    Proper HR policies should be rigidly in place and always followed.

b    Nepotism is wrong, as are 'related-party transactions' such as private consultancy fees paid to a spouse.

c    Staff recruitment by personal word of mouth through family or personal contacts is likely to be wrong.

d    Three-year budget forecasts should be realistic and honest, not disguising problems ahead.

3    **Objective.** School leaders must act and take decisions impartially, fairly and on merit, using the best evidence and without discrimination or bias.

An objective school will design learning outcomes based on evidence. Therefore, all actions should promote the best conditions for all children in the system.

For example:

a    Quick fixes to examination success are illegitimate.

b    Entering children for the higher tier in GCSE mathematics because it is easier to get a threshold grade for the accountability measures but which makes learning maths harder for them is wrong.

4    School leaders are **accountable** to the public for their decisions and actions and must submit themselves to the scrutiny necessary to ensure this.

An accountable school will not seek to subvert, pervert or hide process or outcomes.

Therefore, compliance is not enough: school leaders should interpret accountability measures as being for the good of all children and respond accordingly.

For example, schools should not undermine standards by their behaviour, by creating the conditions in which examination malpractice is expected by exerting unreasonable pressure on junior teachers.

5    School leaders should act and take decisions in an **open** and transparent manner. Information should not be withheld from the public unless there are clear and lawful reasons for so doing.

An open school will be friendly and welcoming. It will explain itself again and again and act upon advice and responses.

Therefore, school leaders should be open to questioning in the way they lead their schools.

For example, they should perform all accountability duties publicly and willingly, keeping governors fully informed and encouraging challenge.

6   School leaders should be truthful.

An **honest** school hides nothing and admits to its mistakes.

Therefore, school leaders should always be honest about their schools.

For example, misrepresenting one's own or others' results in order to recruit children or receive performance-related pay is wrong.

7   School leaders should exhibit these principles in their own **leadership**. They should actively promote and robustly support the principles and be willing to challenge poor behaviour wherever it occurs.

A school where ethical leadership is taken seriously will have leaders at all levels who abide by its principles.

Therefore, school leaders will set a good example in their communities of children, staff, parents and governors. Crucially, they should not set an example of selfishness, unreliability, subjectivity, deviousness or untrustworthiness.

We could pick other virtues or values to replace the ones above. We'd be able to fit the challenges and opportunities of current and historical processes of school accountability into them and we'd end up at the same conclusion. School leaders should be trustworthy, effective and sensible. They should tell the truth and respond to accountability measures for the good of the whole system and in the spirit in which they were instituted. They should expect to be paid in accordance with what the public purse can afford and according to guidelines it lays down. They should serve the interests of the good state by providing the circumstances in which children may become good citizens. They should be dependable in all things and this should be verified by the accountability structures of the state.

# Setting English standards in education

Schools need development or action plans to set their course each year and school leaders are expected to have 'strategic vision' to achieve their aims. The first development plan I ever encountered was as a footsoldier in a tricky spot. 'Here's the school development plan' said the deputy head, waving something at a staff meeting, 'but we're not giving everyone a copy because you wouldn't understand it'. Buy-in from staff was limited.

When I started writing them myself, I began with paradigm statements about what the school should be, and divided them into crunchy tasks to implement and monitor over one or three years. I'd just done this after much thought and consultation in a large and successful school when the Building Schools for the Future (BSF) team arrived.

The BSF programme was predicated on rebuilding struggling schools to give them a fresh start. Mine wasn't struggling in any sense other than having two dilapidated buildings divided by a medieval city. Ready to jump through whatever hoops were presented, I clashed with BSF over development planning. Our plan didn't need rewriting to include BSF buzzwords (including 'innovation' to which, as a school we were pretty allergic). We didn't need rebranding or rebooting, we just needed working heating and lavatories in a watertight building on a single site.

The state needed to fulfil its duty to keep us warm and safe. It needed to trust us to understand our duties and give us an environment fit for the nation's children. It didn't need to use rebuilding to tell us how to think or teach. That's a more complicated job.

In the last chapter I discussed the Principles for Public Life and their use for heads and schools. Education, specifically, is a huge concern of the state and we should look at existing standards built into our schools. What is there?

All qualified teachers in England, at all levels, at all times and in all places have to fulfil the *Teachers' Standards* (2012), which are embedded in their training. They are our single key to a shared understanding of professionalism. The *National Standards of Excellence for Headteachers* of 2015, by contrast, are not mandatory, but used for guidance.

However, both have been produced with the profession by the Department for Education, so they articulate the profession's self-understanding and the expectations that the state has of the teaching profession as a whole, and headteachers in particular.

## The *Teachers' Standards* (2012)

The 'Preamble' to the *Teachers' Standards* (2012) gives a clear overview:

> Teachers make the education of their pupils their first concern, and are accountable for achieving the highest possible standards in work and conduct. Teachers act with honesty and integrity; have strong subject knowledge, keep their knowledge and skills as teachers up-to-date and are self-critical; forge positive professional relationships; and work with parents in the best interests of their pupils.
>
> (Department for Education 2012: 10)

After that it is divided into two parts. Part One has eight subsections, each of which is expanded in the text. Teachers must:

1   Set high expectations which inspire, motivate and challenge pupils

2   Promote good progress and outcomes by pupils

3   Demonstrate good subject and curriculum knowledge

4   Plan and teach well-structured lessons

5   Adapt teaching to respond to the strengths and needs of all

6   Make accurate and productive use of assessment

7   Manage behaviour effectively to ensure a good and safe learning

8   Fulfil wider professional responsibilities

The Standards are task-oriented and clear, which is good. New teachers need to be certain about the high standards expected of them, and it is a good teacher indeed who can fulfil all of them: the Standards are good for the profession. They are generally about *doing*, rather than *being*, though four of them hint at desirable characteristics:

■ Standard 1 requires teachers to *demonstrate consistently the positive attitudes, values and behaviour which are expected of pupils.*

■ Standard 2 requires teachers to *encourage pupils to take a responsible and conscientious attitude to their own work and study.*

■ Standard 4 requires teachers *to promote a love of learning and children's intellectual curiosity.*

■ Standard 7 requires teachers to *take responsibility for promoting good and courteous behaviour.*

Standard 1 requires teachers to model what they expect of pupils, which echoes my contention that teachers and heads are role models at the same time as being public servants. If that is the case, we can say with confidence that all teachers should be

✓ positive

✓ good

✓ responsible

✓ conscientious

✓ intellectually curious

✓ well-mannered

Part Two is altogether different, much shorter and deals with *'personal and professional conduct'*.

> A teacher is expected to demonstrate consistently high standards of personal and professional conduct. The following statements define the behaviour and attitudes which set the required standard for conduct throughout a teacher's career.
>
> (Department for Education 2012: 15)

This has seven brief points, which I include in full.

> Teachers uphold public trust in the profession and maintain high standards of ethics and behaviour, within and outside school, by:

■ treating pupils with dignity, building relationships rooted in mutual respect, and at all times observing proper boundaries appropriate to a teacher's professional position

■ having regard for the need to safeguard pupils' well-being, in accordance with statutory provisions

■ showing tolerance of and respect for the rights of others

■ not undermining fundamental British values, including democracy, the rule of law, individual liberty and mutual respect, and tolerance of those with different faiths and beliefs

- ensuring that personal beliefs are not expressed in ways which exploit pupils' vulnerability or might lead them to break the law

- teachers must have proper and professional regard for the ethos, policies and practices of the school in which they teach, and maintain high standards in their own attendance and punctuality

- teachers must have an understanding of, and always act within, the statutory frameworks which set out their professional duties and responsibilities

(Department for Education 2012: 15)

From these one might also extract characteristics of the 'high standards of ethics':

- trustworthiness

- respectfulness

- kindness

- professionalism

- loyalty

Interestingly, five aspects of 'specific terminology' are also defined, two of which are worth closer attention.

- 'Fundamental British values' is taken from the definition of extremism as articulated in the new Prevent Strategy, which was launched in June 2011. It includes 'democracy, the rule of law, individual liberty and mutual respect and tolerance of different faiths and beliefs'.

(Department for Education 2015b: 5)

Prevent is a very particular strategy for a set of specific and troubling events in current history. Prevent itself is no clearer on the oft-derided 'fundamental British values', which also, in their definition above, form part of the school inspection schedule.

- 'School' means whatever educational setting the standards are applied in. The standards are required to be used by teachers in maintained schools and nonmaintained special schools. Use of the standards in academies and free schools depends on the specific establishment arrangements of those schools. Independent schools are not required to use the standards, but may do so if they wish.

(Department for Education 2012: 9)

This dilutes the Standards more than somewhat. A child is a child, and his education is at the choice of his parents. Why should so many institutions be able to opt out of a very simple, uncontroversial and clear definition of what a child might have the right to expect from his teachers?

I will return to our developing list of desirable characteristics – virtues – later in this chapter.

## National Standards of Excellence for Headteachers (2015)

The *National Standards of Excellence for Headteachers* (2015) are not mandatory but set out to:

> define high standards which are applicable to all headteacher roles within a self-improving school system. These standards are designed to inspire public confidence in headteachers, raise aspirations, secure high academic standards in the nation's schools, and empower the teaching profession.
>
> (Department for Education 2015a: 4)

They are designed to be used by headteachers for their own practice and professional development, by governors and others for appraisal, recruitment, appointment and in school to provide a framework for training middle and senior leaders who aspire to headship. They are built upon the Teachers' Standards *Personal and Professional Code of Conduct*. This applies to all teachers and provides *a foundation upon which the standards for headteachers are built.*

The Preamble to the *National Standards of Excellence for Headteachers* gives a brief overview of the role of the headteacher:

> Headteachers occupy an influential position in society and shape the teaching profession. They are lead professionals and significant role models within the communities they serve. The values and ambitions of headteachers determine the achievements of schools. They are accountable for the education of current and future generations of children. Their leadership has a decisive impact on the quality of teaching and pupils' achievements in the nation's classrooms.
>
> Headteachers lead by example the professional conduct and practice of teachers in a way that minimises unnecessary teacher workload and leaves room for high quality continuous professional development for staff. They secure a climate for the exemplary behaviour of pupils. They set standards and expectations for high academic standards within and beyond their own schools, recognising differences and respecting cultural diversity within contemporary Britain. Headteachers, together with those responsible for governance, are guardians of the nation's schools.
>
> (Department for Education 2015a: 4)

What characteristics may we extract from this comprehensive overview? Headteachers occupy an *influential position in society.* They are *significant role models.* They are *accountable* and with governors *are guardians of the nation's schools.* There are no further virtues identified other than those which may be assumed from the Teacher Standards.

The *National Standards of Excellence for Headteachers* are set out in four 'domains' following the Preamble.

There are four 'Excellence As Standard' domains:

■ Qualities and knowledge

■ Pupils and staff

■ Systems and process

■ The self-improving school system

Within each domain there are six key characteristics expected of the nation's headteachers.

(Department for Education 2015a: 5)

Looking at them closely and combining similar terms, we find the following characteristics therein.

■ accountability (four times)

■ integrity (three times)

■ equality (three times)

■ transparency (three times)

■ optimism

■ creativity

■ resilience

■ astuteness

■ calm

■ rigorousness

■ entrepreneurialism

■ innovation

■ inspirational

We would expect to see *accountability* dominate government-issue standards. Two of the three other repeat characteristics also found in the Standards for Public Life – *integrity* and *openness* (transparency). There is much reference to managerial characteristics such as *calmness* and the ability to *inspire*. There are buzzwords of the educational zeitgeist such as *entrepreneurialism, innovation* and *'excellence'* itself. We meet our old friends: *moral purpose* and *resilience* again.

What we don't find very clearly are virtues in the Aristotelian sense. Virtues can help the state to trust teachers and headteachers, and might render the creation of such standards less necessary. Notice: there is much on *safeguarding*, but <u>kindness</u> is unnamed. There is plenty of *accountability* but no <u>honesty</u>. There is *astuteness*, but not <u>wisdom</u>.

It is reasonable to assume that those who devised that standards took it for granted that teachers and headteachers are, personally, good people with the right intention. Therefore, as long as they fulfil their tasks conscientiously they may be entrusted with stewardship of the next generation. The risk of overlooking virtue in these formulations is simple and troubling. In a standards-driven workforce, anything not specified may not be valued, and anything not prohibited may be permissible.

Setting standards for these most important of roles is a legitimate and sensible exercise of the state's authority and care for its young. Reading the two sets of standards alone, however, it might be possible to argue that those entrusted with the nation's young have only to be learned, effective, conscientious and accountable. Without wishing to be melodramatic, there have been times in living history when such characteristics were also deemed sufficient. They are not enough to expect of those entrusted with our children.

How might we underpin these hopeful edifices with strong foundations in virtue?

# Part 3
# Why is it difficult to agree about good educational leadership?

# 10 Perverse accountability

Accountability pressures cause interesting decisions. I was a headteacher in the notorious Durham Fish Oil Trial of 2007. Led by a respected Educational Psychologist and the County Chief Schools Inspector, this scheme gave expensive fish oil capsules to children to see if their learning and test scores improved.

The first trial focused on improving behaviour and reducing exclusions among a targeted group of children with ADHD. The second project was a county-wide fish-oil bonanza to improve results. Schools and parents signed up to giving children regular fish oil, despite logistical difficulties. It was pilloried in the press, tenaciously by Ben Goldacre in The Guardian, as bad science. No controls, no proper scrutiny, no adequate reporting, too much commercial interest.

I took a relaxed view. I reckoned that fish oil is generally believed to be important to the diet. It is at worst harmless and at best might actually do children some good. The pills were pricey in the shops but the project gave them to poor children. It might make them healthier. I could live with the bad science, though this quite reasonably infuriated the staffroom mathematicians, scientists and sociologists.

The Oxford University website Practical Ethics reflected thus:

> . . . the greatest annoyance with the whole affair is that it missed the chance of doing good research on an important question. There are reasons to think certain fatty acids can have a positive effect on developing brains. If they have, the social gains of ensuring adequate uptake could be very large. Yet we have very little solid data. This is something the Durham study could have helped answer. Now the most likely result will be bringing the area into disrepute.

Fish Oil was one project in the heyday of outcomes-led bad science in schools. Enthusiastic adopting of snake oil techniques like thinking hats, brain gym and multiple intelligences all brought teaching into disrepute. Contemporary with the use of GCSE equivalences in performance tables, the backlash came in a reaction which changed the world for the better: better curricula and proper research, embedded in schools.

If we wanted to try such a project now, we could call upon researchers who are ready to work with schools and we could measure the effects on achievement much more accurately. If we were used to the kind of thinking required by the ethical leadership framework – of openness, wisdom and service – we might plan it better and be more cagey about fixes designed to inflate outcomes.

Was the Fish Oil Trial worth it? Perhaps not. As a professional exercise it was clumsy and lacked research expertise. Its constraints were huge and its benefits tiny. Its proponents, however, were good people who'd devoted their adult lives to the service of children, particularly poor children in an area of massive social disadvantage. They took their responsibilities *in loco parentis* very seriously. They should have done it better, but the opprobrium heaped upon them seemed unjust, from people who'd never raised a finger to help the former pit villages.

There was little public debate then about the perverse incentives of the performance tables. It was easy to rubbish the lengths to which good people would go to meet accountability measures which often benefitted the better-off and exposed those who served the poor to ridicule. But someone has to feed the children better. Where lay the fault?

In 2017, Geoff Barton, the new General Secretary of the Association of School and College Leaders (ASCL), began to talk about the work of ASCL's Ethical Leadership Commission as he went from place to place. He had consistently similar replies from school leaders, the most optimistic example of which was from Leeds in November 2017:

> We love what you're saying about being ethical leaders, but the accountability system makes it so difficult to do.

As he said: 'what an indictment.'

## Accountability

Schools should be accountable. As I discussed earlier, schools should be accountable to the children they serve, the parents who entrust us *in loco parentis*, and the state. They should be accountable to the communities in which they are placed, to the taxpayers who fund them and the wider democracy. That accountability should be robust. Weak accountability would mean that no one knew what schools were doing, why or how. It might lead to a disparaging of children (as shiftless), schooling (in chaos) and teachers (as useless). Accountability is both right and good: the serious act of a mature and stable state.

School accountability should therefore demonstrate that schools provide what is right for the child, what the careful parent would want and what the state has defined. Its outputs should demonstrate that children are being kept safe and learning what the state wants them to learn by the actions of well-qualified teachers. It should demonstrate that children are effectively prepared to be useful, self-supporting adult citizens.

These are rather abstract aims, but proxies make them manageable. We have expectations of safeguarding, audit, and teacher qualifications. From the ancient Mandarins to the 16-year-old chewing his pen, we have used standardised examination to measure learning outcomes. These activities all satisfy Nolan's requirement of objectivity. So why do they fail to guarantee ethical behaviour?

## School performance and examination outcomes

For most of my headship years, accountability for a secondary school was built on the 5A* – C GCSE measure. In this, a school's success was judged on the aggregated success of its children. To safeguard performance in the published data tables, heads made sure that every child who could possibly get five C grades got them. The measure itself was devalued by 'equivalent' qualifications, often very easy or formulaic courses, and teacher-assessed or teacher-supported coursework.

In order to place this crude threshold measure in the differing context of schools, in the interests of justice, a 'contextual value-added' score (CVA) was added. Mitigating factors such as SEN, birth month, gender, ethnicity and language were factored into a combined score centred on 1000 so that the endeavour of schools in challenging circumstances of communities would not be undervalued. Subsequently, the measure changed to 5A* – CEM, valuing English and maths, and CVA was abandoned as a potentially limiting measure.

However, schools had tooled themselves up to provide the A* – C yields given the best rating by the state. Curricula were restricted and GCSE options both prescribed and proscribed for children according to their likelihood of success. The most successful schools and heads were publicly lauded. At the same time, deregulation in the system offered inducements for schools to become independent, academies freed from the strictures of the state, including in the setting of salaries.

By the time of writing, perverse accountability had become partially synonymous for accountability itself in schools. Whenever a new measure is devised and introduced, school leaders think hard and gaze into the middle distance. How will this affect me? What picture will this paint of my school? How will it be enforced? How may I avoid catastrophe? A measure is no sooner introduced objectively to measure part of a school's provision than school leaders change their schools to focus on it. Campbell's Law (1979) argues that accountability measures tend to skew the metric upon which they rest and this has also been true for schools. Accountability drives how schools work.

Nolan's formulation of accountability suggests that school accountability should arise naturally out of the good provision of the school. Judgements should be in accordance with what that provision demonstrates.

However, proxy accountability measurements protect the public's expenditure and set reasonable targets for the state's provision and intervention. We have national averages and expectations, audit, baselines and floor targets. All these are the reasonable furnishings of the concerned state and in a well-developed system, intervention should be, as Tony Blair said, in inverse proportion to need.

So, if the accountability is fair why might a committed, resourceful and highly-educated workforce end up rendering them perverse? Why is there a mismatch between the logical approach of the regulators and the anxious responses of the senior professionals? Why, for example, does one regulator find it necessary regularly to publish 'myth-busters'? (Ofsted 2018).

Permit me to posit 10 reasons for this discord.

1 **We mistake our proxies for our goals.** All the measurements we take of schools are to promote a good national compulsory education system in an advanced democracy. We benchmark ourselves against other countries and equate their prosperity or lack of it with their educational standards or lack of them. The frequent changes of political intervention in the Department for Education mean that a long-term development plan to such end can hardly be established as our adversarial politics require change from one party's programmes to another. Therefore, an international *reductio ad absurdum* obtains along the lines of: 'Chinese children are better at maths than English children and the Chinese economy is booming. Also, there are a lot of Chinese people. To sustain our economy, competitiveness and success as a nation, English children must become better at maths until they can compete with Chinese children.' Examination results represent mathematical ability, so the results must be raised. Individual schools' curricula may therefore be ineffectively affected to respond to global over-simplification.

2 **We use the same measurements for children's progress and school effectiveness.** In order for a school to be successful it has to have individually successful children. Therefore low-achieving or slow-acquiring children are a high-stakes problem, but both must be fixed inside the time window that allows an average child to make average progress. The accountability measures may not offer enough time for Delilah to grasp trigonometry before she's 16 so heads may be tempted to force progress unsustainably, or resort to examination misjudgement.

St Olave's Grammar School in Kent hit the headlines in 2017 when students who didn't meet stringent progression grades to move from Year 12 to Year 13 were told to leave.

The report, commissioned by Bromley Council, challenged the pursuit of academic excellence at all costs. "A school has the responsibility to do its best by all its pupils," the report said. By excluding students the school had put the institution above the pupils, it found. "Parents of the pupils affected were right to say their children were being treated as collateral damage. It should not have happened . . . The report queried [the headteacher's] claims that he did not know the year 13 exclusions were potentially illegal. It is clear that no one told the head that what he was doing was illegal. It is less clear why they didn't. The admissions code and the off-rolling rules are not obscure pieces of legislation."

(*The Guardian*, July 2018)

3 **Progress measures work well at national level but less well at school level and they are a uselessly blunt instrument at child level.** Academically inclined children make better progress than slower-acquirers. Well-off children make better progress than poor children. School leaders may despair of calibrations by which they can never succeed.

4 **Britain's unequal society makes state educators suspicious of the motives and competence of politicians.** They suspect that cabinet members may not be fully conversant with state education, or personally committed to it. This is compounded when politicians seek to intervene in the content or shape of the curriculum, especially when that is explicitly based on politicians' personal experience in selective and fee-paying schools.

5 **School performance language and discourse became overheated and generated a destructive lexicon.** Struggling schools have been castigated as 'failing'. Heads who question feverish political aims are 'enemies of promise'. University education departments are 'the blob'. Excitable reporting feeds an expectation of precipitate action so a school's overseers (academy chain, diocese or Local Authority) may congratulate themselves on 'zero-tolerance' of failure and their commitment to 'sky-high aspirations'. Heads live in fear of losing their jobs as a demonstration of 'decisive action'. They may therefore act to save themselves – or become incapable of rational planning.

6 **Because 'leadership' is set as central to a school's success the head may find herself victim.** In the common parlance this is described as *football manager syndrome*, or heads being 'one poor Ofsted away from a P45'. This has been exacerbated by politicians and regulators using unhelpful analogies for the desired attributes of headteachers: 'battleaxes and bruisers', 'Lone Rangers'. A head struggling to raise results is described as 'weak', to be 'rooted out'. But these public servants have mortgages and children of their own to support: they cannot afford to be sacked so they may take desperate action or not accept egregiously difficult jobs in the first place.

7  **Some kinds of public accountability set schools against one another.** In an area of declining population this may spell closure for a school which loses a publicity battle, whether the schools are comparable or not. School leaders become divided by anger or envy and are unlikely to combine for the greater good of the system. Heads may be tempted to be untruthful about their schools.

8  **The British system is geographically divergent.** Some areas are overpopulated and need as many school places as can be generated. Others are underpopulated so provision needs careful management. Solutions generated in London may not serve the people of Northumberland or Grimsby. Heads may lose confidence that reliable provision is justified and required. They may even have heard it publicly disparaged as 'bog standard'. They may feel compelled to innovate or emulate, to deleterious effect.

9  **In order to solve problems within the life of a single parliament, an unreasonable amount of weight is placed on superficial answers.** Headline-grabbing initiatives become bona fide solutions before any evidence is available of sustainability or success. Longitudinal studies into pet projects are rare. Heads may adopt superficial and unsuccessful solutions to difficult problems.

10  **Regulation is done cheaply by governments determined to reduce public sector spending while claiming to know the strengths and weaknesses of every institution.** Looking deeply at a school takes time and wisdom. Solving a local problem may take years. Training inspectors to be able to do this is expensive and paying them accordingly would cost more. Heads are at the mercy of blunt evaluation tools.

The consequence of these ten problems for schools is clear and depressing, visible in the behaviour of headteachers who find it hard to base their practice on deep ethical values while they fear for their school's and their own professional survival. Children, parents and the state would be better served by longitudinal, accurate and formative accountability measures. In the same way that the taxpayer understands that waiting list times and budget deficits don't measure the value of the NHS, our current accountability metrics don't explain the value and the scope of our schools.

Behaving with integrity under scrutiny in these circumstances requires a strong intrinsic motivation and self-understanding. If we want headteachers to model the behaviour we want for our young, then they must be given the space to do the job thoughtfully and effectively. If we can help heads think the foundations of their decision-making, we could take two big steps into a better future. First, accountability measures would be a true and honest reflection of education. Second, we would set a much better example to our children.

Accountability is not enough. We have to do good.

# What should we do? Using ethics to make better decisions

'The cult of the macho "strong leader", which dominates education, has been damaging in so many ways. I always seem to be reading fatuous accounts of the apparently super-human workloads of our academy Trust principals and university presidents. They rise at 5am to lead their institutions forward with an hour of emails, followed by breakfast meetings, and fall late into bed having worked tirelessly all day for their underlings. It is narcissist guff and to most of us is unimpressive, but given how much educational leaders pay themselves, it is perhaps not surprising that they try to justify their worth in this way.'

(Danny Dorling, Halford Mackinder Professor of Geography, Oxford University. *The Guardian*, 20 March 2018)

As Robert Burns said:

O wad some Power the giftie gie us

To see oursels as ithers see us.

Armed with an understanding of the scope of the headteacher's role and some ethical principles and personal virtues, how might we help busy people make reliably good judgements using common language? In Chapters 13–19 I set out heads' work, explain the scope of heads' decision-making and offer advice on using the Framework for Ethical Leadership.

For experienced heads I offer some dilemmas taken from real life to develop thinking and action. Circumstances and orthodoxies alter, but I have tried to make the dilemmas relatively timeless in educational terms, that is, not linked to the particular focus of a Secretary of State or HMCI, nor the Byzantine affordances of accountability measures. (The latter are particularly prone to being affected not only by political imperatives, but by the development of statistical software. This I cannot foresee.)

Many, or most, dilemmas in school require, as Fullan (2015) observed, decisions to be taken in situations of unavoidable ambiguity. Professionals should be able to cope with this and have the resources ready to think through, process, deliberate and tackle a problem. This chapter offers examples of using the mapping of the ethical code and navigating with a moral compass. This is not the same as individuals asserting personal 'moral purpose'. Our professional responsibility to children, society and one another requires us to recognise and share a common purpose, and honourable intent.

## The tools for the job

Key concepts:

1   Schools are where the nation looks after its young.

2   School leaders are simultaneously good public servants and good role models.

3   School leaders are professionals working with and for children and the state *in loco parentis*.

4   Professionals require consent, experience constraint, use expertise and bring public benefit.

5   Ethical thinking uses rights, duties, virtues and cases.

6   The Principles for Public Life are selflessness, openness, objectivity, accountability, honesty, integrity and leadership.

7   The virtues of the Ethical Framework are trust, wisdom, kindness, justice, service, courage and optimism.

8   Accountability is not enough. We have to do good.

    . . . because schools are the place where the nation looks after its young.

# 12 The theatre of education

I moved jobs and a fellow head welcomed me warmly. 'Of course, no one's ever heard of you but we looked you up and you seemed to be doing a good job'. I was mildly outraged as well as amused. I'd moved 200 miles or so but I wasn't unknown among educators. And what did it matter? Who said knowing him validated my existence? I'd only met him a month ago.

There's strength in quiet industry and decent human endeavour doesn't need to be a big performance. An Australian colleague and I had been talked at by a government deliverer in the Blair days who'd segued from the officious to the patronising. B's opening remark was 'Son, I taught on three continents before you were born'. Later in a tetchy session reflecting on another's self-promoting TV appearance he just said 'For shame. You give us all a bad name'.

B's later career passed in obscure diligence leading a good school in a dull town. No one had ever heard of him except the generations of families he served. His slap of them both was only partly exasperation. It was eloquently saying – you may be in the papers and heading for knighthoods, mateys, but I've done my best for 40 years. Don't assume I'm not worth listening to, struth.

Success in anything shouldn't be determined by notoriety but the quality of our service.

Before we arrange our tools for the dissection of ethical dilemmas, let us extract the likely causes of difficulty. Using the *National Standards of Excellence for Head-teachers* discussed in Chapter 9, let's look at what heads do all day.

The standards have 'four domains' (perhaps derived from management discourse):

- Qualities and knowledge

- Pupils and staff

■ Systems and process

■ The self-improving school system

However, I think it more helpful to look at them in the language of professional educators.

## The leader as professional

The educational values and ambitions of headteachers and those responsible for governance determine the achievements of schools. Heads are lead professionals in a self-improving school system within and beyond their own schools. They shape and empower the teaching profession.

## The leader in society

Headteachers inspire public confidence in education and occupy an influential position in society. They are guardians of the nation's schools and significant role models within the communities they serve. They are accountable for the education of current and future generations of children. They understand and respect the differences and cultural diversity within contemporary Britain.

## The leader and the child

Their leadership enables exemplary behaviour of pupils. It has a decisive impact on quality of teaching. Thus, they raise expectations and aspirations, and secure high academic standards in the nation's schools and classrooms.

Teachers are engaged in the quotidian tasks of the *Teachers' Standards*, of:

1   Setting high expectations

2   Promoting good progress

3   Demonstrating good knowledge

4   Planning and teaching well-structured lessons

5   Adapting teaching to respond to all

6   Making accurate and use of assessment

7   Managing behaviour

8   Fulfilling wider professional responsibilities

They are also engaged in the personal responsibilities of Part Two of the standards. Therefore, we may assume that the eight above are all subsumed into heads' and governors' responsibilities.

Compared to our earlier exploration of school leaders' responsibilities, there is one area missing. That is the duty of the school leader to and as a parent, *in loco parentis* on behalf of the state. Perhaps that is why the standards read a little coldly. It is not just that they are not very elegant examples of Civil Service English, but that they miss an aspect of the job that makes it supremely captivating, irritating and worth doing.

There is that world of human struggle buried beneath the simple phrases: love, sacrifice, endurance, honour, fear, commitment, determination, sleepless nights, and sometimes impotent rage on behalf of the nation's children. The standards are clear, but they require a foundation of steel and humanity to make them work for the good and not just for the moment. How might we build this foundation?

The next chapters deal with language, training and structure. Let's look at:

- language to tackle ethical issues and its use;

- training and development for school leaders to help them tackle ethical issues;

- a way of structuring the encountering of dilemmas in our professional system.

# Part 4
# The Framework for Ethical Educational Leadership 2018

# 13 A Framework for Ethical Educational Leadership 2018

> I was brought up in the voluntary sector tradition and fully trained in committee procedure by the time I was 16. This Commission was the most daunting of all. The great and the good responded to the call, we had nine meetings to set out our hopes and plans and after that, a language to promote and a new way of thinking about school leadership. For me it was terrifying, exhausting and wonderful, just like being a headteacher.

The Association of School and College Leaders, ASCL, is a Trade Union and professional association for school leaders, of which I have been a member since first becoming a deputy head in 1997. ASCL was concerned about the enormous pressure that high-stakes accountability was exerting on its members. This was shown not just in the number of premature departures from school leadership but also from personal professional difficulties in which an increasing number of members found themselves entangled. *Member Support* records showed a steady upward trend and there were frequent lurid press stories about school leaders behaving badly.

ASCL's decision-making body, ASCL Council, agreed that practical and analytic ethics needed exploring and explaining. At the 2017 Annual Conference we announced the start of a year-long project to develop principles for ethical educational leadership : '*to help leaders navigate the educational moral maze*'.

I chaired the *Ethical Leadership Commission* (ELC) we set up to do this work. I hoped from that position to be able to make a difference to the way school leaders understand the scope of their roles, and to open up debate on their responsibility in and to society as a whole. That I may also have been motivated by furious discontent at the lexicon of school leadership discourse may reasonably be inferred from preceding chapters.

Trying to express a complex area simply, ASCL explained:

We face ethical dilemmas every day but we don't have an agreed framework that enables us to explore and test them against ethical principles in a safe space.

(ASCL Ethical Leadership Commission 2018: 1)

A 'safe space' being a space away from the regulators. It was crucially important to ASCL that our ethical debate should be looking to support and guide rather than identify and blame, and that hope for a better future rather than picking over a compromised past would be our focus.

The ELC was made up of senior postholders from major stakeholders in education at the time. (The organisations are listed at the end of this chapter). It aimed to develop principles to set out our expectations of school leaders' own behaviour and the example of good behaviour that we should set to children and our communities. We hoped to:

■ embed the language of ethics in leadership discourse as well as in all teacher and school leader training through our **Framework for Ethical Education Leadership**;

■ design participatory opportunities to help such reflection and embolden school leaders to discuss human virtues as well as the personal motivations beloved of leadership training;

■ improve the conditions for discussing wise and successful leadership, by setting up a reference point for ethically difficult issues for the profession.

Our initial focus was on the language of ethical educational leadership. We agreed that shared ethical standards should not be taken for granted. Differences in age, background and culture mean that 'unwritten' rules might act as barriers to quality rather than its guarantors. Explicit standards might help leaders be accountable for their actions and hold others to the same standards.

The ELC based its proposal on the **Principles for Public Life**, first set out in 1995 and which have applied to anyone working as a 'public office-holder' since 2013. We discarded the idea of a code of ethics, mindful of the dangers of tacit acceptance but actual indifference. As I discussed in Chapter 10, school leadership is beset with quality standards, performance indicators and other tick-box processes. Taking advice from those involved both in regulation and in ethical development outside education, we developed a framework, not a checklist.

If I may remind readers of the aims of the Principles for Public Life? They are *selflessness, integrity, objectivity, accountability, openness, honesty and leadership*:

Holders of public office should exhibit these principles in their own behaviour. They should actively promote and robustly support the principles and be willing to challenge poor behaviour wherever it occurs.

(Committee on Standards in Public Life 1995)

After lengthy debate, the ELC proposed that it was in an expansion of the catch-all **'leadership'** that our proposed virtues should lie.

> Schools serve children and young people and help them grow into fulfilled and useful citizens. As role models for young people how we behave as leaders is as important as what we do. Leaders should show leadership through the following personal characteristics or virtues.
>
> 1 TRUST
>
> 2 WISDOM
>
> 3 KINDNESS
>
> 4 JUSTICE
>
> 5 SERVICE
>
> 6 COURAGE
>
> 7 OPTIMISM
>
> (ASCL Ethical Leadership Commission 2018: 5)

We hoped that the Framework would give clear structure to what most teachers and headteachers know intuitively. We hoped that it would help them make good decisions for the good of our profession, children, communities and the state.

## Professional development for ethical professionals

ASCL's advocacy of the programme required a commitment to embed ethical leadership at the heart of its advocacy and advice. We hoped to include the language of ethics in member support, publishing annual reports on ethical dilemmas faced by ASCL members.

However, our scope was much broader. We wanted to embed the Framework so that a consistent ethical leadership message could develop across the sector.

We want to see:

- Widespread use of the values and virtues language of the Framework.

- Ethics input into teacher and leader training programmes at all levels.

- A long-term space for ethical debate, led and moderated by a successor body to the ELC on similar lines to the Committee for Standards in Public Life. This should include consideration of the potential effects of policy and accountability changes on school leaders' behaviour in advance of changes.

The ELC hoped that adopting a **Framework for Ethical Educational Leadership** might be a source of unity for schools and trusts in a deregulated, fragmented system.

We devised a short introduction to embedding ethics in action for governors (below), encouraging them to develop a **statement of ethical educational leadership principles** as a touchstone for their own decisions, helping them monitor and sustain their own good practice. While definitively avoiding any involvement in regulation or sanction, we hoped that the Framework might give language to worried colleagues, perhaps clarify whistleblowing and assist the advice and support structures of professional associations.

## The Framework for Ethical Educational Leadership

*Ethical educational leadership is based upon the Seven Principles for Public Life.*

1   **Selflessness**

Leaders should act solely in the interest of children and young people.

2   **Integrity**

Leaders must avoid placing themselves under any obligation to people or organisations that might try inappropriately to influence them in their work. Before acting or taking decisions they must declare and resolve openly any perceived conflict of interest and relationships.

3   **Objectivity**

Leaders must act and take decisions impartially and fairly, using the best evidence and without discrimination or bias. Leaders should be dispassionate, exercising judgement and analysis for the good of children and young people.

4   **Accountability**

Leaders are accountable to the public for their decisions and actions and must submit themselves to the scrutiny necessary to ensure this.

5   **Openness**

Leaders should act and take decisions in an open and transparent manner. Information should not be withheld from scrutiny unless there are clear and lawful reasons for so doing.

6   **Honesty**

Leaders should be truthful.

7   **Leadership**

Leaders should exhibit these principles in their own behaviour. They should actively promote and robustly support the principles and be willing to challenge poor behaviour wherever it occurs. Leaders include both those who are paid to lead schools and those who volunteer to govern them.

*Schools and colleges serve children and young people and help them grow into fulfilled and valued citizens. As role models for the young, how we behave as leaders is as important as what we do Leaders should show leadership through the following personal characteristics or virtues.*

**Trust:** leaders are trustworthy and reliable. We hold trust on behalf of children and should be beyond reproach. We are honest about our motivations.

**Wisdom:** leaders use experience, knowledge and insight. We demonstrate moderation and self-awareness. We act calmly and rationally. We serve with propriety and good sense.

**Kindness**: leaders demonstrate respect, generosity of spirit and good temper. We give difficult messages humanely where conflict is unavoidable.

**Justice:** leaders are fair and work for the good of all children. We seek to enable all young people to lead useful, happy and fulfilling lives.

**Service:** leaders are conscientious and dutiful. We demonstrate humility and self-control, supporting the structures, conventions and rules which safeguard quality. Our actions protect high-quality education.

**Courage**: leaders work courageously in the best interests of children and young people. We protect their safety and their right to a broad, effective and creative education. We hold one another to account courageously.

**Optimism:** leaders are positive and encouraging. Despite difficulties and pressures we are developing excellent education to change the world for the better.

It is upon this small but mighty human foundation that the ELC also hoped to change the educational world for the better.

## Participating organisations in the Ethical Leadership Commission

- ASCL

- The National Association of Head Teachers (the primary-phase-focused association)

- Ofsted

- University College London's Institute of Education

- The Headmasters' and Headmistresses' Conference

- Freedom and Autonomy for Schools National Association (focusing on free schools and academies)

- The Chartered College of Teachers

- The Foundation for Leadership in Education

- The Committee for Standards in Public Life

- The Church of England Education Department

- The International Confederation of Principals

- The National Governance Association

- The Teaching Schools Council

- Ambition School Leadership (a training and development charity for teachers and leaders)

- 'The Corporate Philosopher

# Using the Framework for Ethical Educational Leadership

**14**

## Selflessness and pay

**Selflessness:** Leaders should act solely in the interest of children and young people.

> A CEO/Executive Principal in a Multi-Academy Trust of two secondary schools and four primary schools has an annual salary of £210k, plus pension, company car and private medical scheme. Performance management is arranged so that there is an annual bonus available for meeting targets negotiated similarly to the HTPM scheme. While holiday time is negotiable (35 days + Bank Holidays); some of it may be taken in term time. The CEO is paid £120k more than the next highest paid employee of the MAT. A parent has written to ask the Trust to justify this remuneration package.

## Context

It may be very British not to discuss one's salary. Those paid from the public purse, however, cannot expect to be quite so coy. State education was built on public sector pay agreements which gave transparency. It was possible to compare the pay of school leaders with each other. They could also be compared to senior police officers, for example, or doctors. Colleagues inside an institution could rest assured that published pay structures guaranteed relatively equal pay for equal work. The head's salary was agreed by governors using a public calculation, ratified by local government.

Schools leaving Local Authority control could ignore old structures and set pay differently. Deregulation of all pay scales gave every teacher the right to negotiate his or her worth – especially at times of teacher and school leader shortage. Salaries for heads and CEOs (and university Vice-Chancellors) were the subject of press scrutiny.

Seeing huge salaries in business and elsewhere, teachers and heads began to argue for the kind of benefits the chap at the dinner lectured me about, based on the notion of personal worth 'because we're worth it'. That's not how it works, and those who choose to work for the state must expect the constraints that brings.

As a branch Secretary for ASCL I was asked many questions I couldn't answer. One that I could answer, but not politely, was 'I've achieved so much. Is there any way I can give myself a decent pay rise without staff knowing?'

Your salary and your school's pay structure requires **selflessness:** *putting the needs of the children – the school – first.*

**Points to consider:**

■ Each child has a right to a decent education led by quality professionals who are valued by the state. Pay negotiated at local level risks chasms opening up between schools who can afford to pay well and schools who can't. It locks teachers into staying in richer schools.

■ Market forces do not guarantee that poor children, whose progress is more diffi-cult to guarantee, will be served by the best leaders if there is no national mod-erating of pay.

■ Avarice, self-importance and secrecy are poor role models for children.

■ Governors do not have magic money trees.

**An ethical leader will ask:**

1   Why is the CEO paid so much? Are pension benefits on top of this? What is his security of tenure? Potential severance terms? What is the precise nature of his extra responsibilities or workload, qualifications or expertise, in public sector terms?

2   Does the Trust have an independent Remuneration Committees committed to the Principles for Public Life? Has the Trust benchmarked CEO pay with local posts of similar size and responsibility?

3   Is there evidence of equal pay for equal work in the Trust?

4   Does everyone concerned in a school understand the principles used in their pay determination including pension benefits?

5   What is the benefit to the schools and the children of this level of pay? What economies are being made elsewhere in order to pay this salary?

**An ethical leader will:**

1   Reform the pay structure within the Trust so that future remuneration is moderated.

2   Assess the benefit of all aspects of the salary package and take steps to maxi-mise public benefit.

# Honesty and examinations

You're a head and your son is at school in the next town. He comes home after a GCSE and explains that there was a mistake on the paper and the head of maths had to explain what the question really meant to the candidates in the hall. You're surprised you didn't hear of this from your own exam room and you've woken at 0500 thinking about it.

**Honesty:** leaders should be truthful.

## Context

Examination results are the measure of a child's achievement at school. They should be calibrated so that diligent children with all speeds of knowledge acquisition may be congratulated on a job well done after so many years of compulsory education.

Examinations in the English system are used simultaneously to measure the performance of the child and the school. The specification and examination are provided by competing commercial organisations. Accountability pressure has led to unfortunate practices such as 'teaching to the test' to maximise results, which reduces the child's access to knowledge. It may also have led to unacceptable practices which examination boards calmly call 'malpractice and irregularity'.

High-stakes accountability measures and febrile discussion of results as a proxy for a child's worth (to family or the economy) make examination malpractice more likely. So, examination conduct should be rigorous and effectively monitored. Practices such as coursework which advantage a child with involved parents over a child having to fend for himself should be removed from the system. Practices relying on robust teacher assessment and moderation are acceptable – with suitable measures to guarantee good conduct. Practices which advantage one centre's candidates over another – like having a difficult question explained to them and the solution suggested – are malpractice.

Examination results must be accurate and reliable. They are a proxy for education, not its goal. They should be achieved with **honesty.**

**Points to consider:**

- Each child has a right to a reliable and nationally standardised examination result. Exam malpractice undermines the entire system. Heads of Centres uphold the system/

- Subject leads and teachers are clearly trained by the examination boards in acceptable conduct. There is no room for doubt.

- A Head of Centre relies on subject leadership to know and do the right thing.

- The Examinations Officer would know that teachers may not be in the examination room once the paper has started.
- Subject leaders may argue with some vehemence that 'everybody does it'.

**An ethical leader will ask:**

1   Did it happen? As a parent she should ring the head. If that doesn't put her mind at rest she may consider whistleblowing to the examination board. This may endanger her own son's grade.

2   Could it happen here? She'll look to her own school too: is any irregularity investigated in school as directed by the examination board, and reported fully to governors?

**An ethical leader will:**

1   Ensure that examination requirements are followed exactly.

2   Refer herself to the examinations board if there is any doubt.

3   Give the Examinations Officer sufficient status so that rules are followed, for the good of all children.

## Openness and governance

**Openness:** Leaders should act and take decisions in an open and transparent manner. Information should not be withheld from scrutiny unless there are clear and lawful reasons for so doing.

Your Trust has grown well and the trustees now in place are a visionary group. This is good, because there have been three CEOs and three Chairs of Trustees in the last five years and the whole enterprise has taken some time to find its way. Freed from the poor-quality advice they believed Local Authority Clerks gave, local governors have been equipped with trust clerking and follow central standards. These standards have taken some time to agree on, with the turnover of CEOs, and there has been a higher than usual turnover of governors and trustees.

Trustees are now very keen to make sure that their vision is promoted in their schools. On a strategy day together they produced two documents: their procedures for intervening at classroom and parent level, and the vision they'll look for in recruiting new governors. As an EH in the Trust you're worried about their approach.

## Context

Governors join schools from all walks of life. They bring vital experience of the world and society beyond the gate. Their intelligence and commitment act as foil and stimulus to professional leadership.

Ethical governance dilemmas present themselves when governors seek to act beyond the strategic. They may be tempted to exert undue influence on the operational work of the school or Trust. This may be caused by their own motivations or community pressures.

Governance can itself be compromised when professional school leaders use boards for rubber-stamping, or seek to evade governors' legitimate scrutiny.

If a governor is motivated by personal power or seeks to represent a particular family or interest group then it is unlikely that equality will be best served. Such interference will not model virtuous character.

If governors or trusts only seek to replicate their own approach, motivations and beliefs when recruiting fellows, that may lead to complacency and assumed agreement that do not serve the state well.

Accountability as well as openness expects governors to be open to scrutiny from regulators and system managers, and also from the community served by the school or Trust.

Each child has a right to the best possible education. The providers of this education are the trained and accredited professionals. The child's education should not be improved and not impeded by the governors. This is the case for all children in all schools.

**Points to consider:**

■ Trustees and governors are crucial in a school's life. They are responsible for the public assets the school holds, its budget and its success.

■ Governors sometimes find it challenging to lift their heads from the daily issues of the school and think strategically. They have to be helped to do this by skilled leadership, including that of the professionals running the schools.

■ Governors need to be open. A clear description of what they'd like in new governors shouldn't tip over into a blueprint that means every governor has the same background or viewpoint.

■ Governors are not teachers or inspectors. They must trust the professionals to report honestly on what's happening in classrooms.

**An ethical leader will ask:**

1   Are governors thoroughly trained in their duties and the principles underlying them?

2   Is there an objective and public programme of work for them to do so that they may be enabled to think broadly and accurately about the school or Trust's performance?

3   Are governors outward-facing and well informed about the education world?

4   Do they work with professional leaders to develop scrutiny tools suitable for the school?

5   Do governors respect confidentiality and collective decision-making?

**An ethical leader will:**

1   Encourage governors and trustees to be fully trained in the scope of their role: the NGA has helpful programmes for this.

2   Encourage governors and trustees systematically to make sure that they represent the communities they serve.

3   Encourage governors to adopt the Ethical Leadership Framework.

## Staffing and objectivity

**Objectivity:** leaders must act and take decisions impartially and fairly, using the best evidence and without discrimination or bias. Leaders should be dispassionate, exercising judgement and analysis for the good of children and young people.

> The advantage of a big MAT model is that the supply of good teachers and leaders is very reliable. If you train your own good NQTs and keep them, then you can promote as required through the group, including to Heads of School posts. Sometimes you need to advertise externally, for shortage subjects. Salaries are by negotiation, depending on the state of the market.
>
> You work them hard and discourage good ones from leaving and have occasionally threatened to give an inaccurately poor reference. Nonetheless, you're surprised by the number of teachers who leave after five or so years and how many of them leave teaching altogether.
>
> In looking over the MAT's Public Sector Equality Duty requirement, you wonder if your process is scalable across the country. Are you contributing to improving teacher recruitment and retention, or not? You'll put it to the board that senior posts as well as the more junior should be advertised publicly.

Good teachers are required for all children in all schools. Salary 'flexibilities' can lead to widely differing terms and conditions for teachers. Good teachers will stay in schools where they are treated fairly and where finances allow for better terms and conditions.

The fair treatment of teachers and school staff should be taken for granted in a model community. However, high-stakes accountability, some management styles and squeezed funding has led to poor outcomes for many teachers. Increased teaching loads, larger classes, anxious leaders, frozen pay and reduced influence of the teacher unions have changed the weather, especially for teachers. Many thousands have left the service and too few recruits join it.

Every child deserves a good education from well-qualified professionals with job security. This means that good learning and memorable experiences can be built up and refined. Exhausted, unhappy and resentful teachers can have as negative an effect on children's learning and happiness as poorly qualified and temporary ones. Virtuous character is modelled to children by the kind and fair treatment of colleagues in an organisation, so an **objective** leader must act and take decisions impartially and fairly.

**Points to consider:**

■ All employees should be treated fairly and in accordance with the law.

■ Schools should participate in creating and retaining a high-quality, happy workforce, nationally.

■ Schools are different. Teachers trained in a very particular manner may not have broader transferable skills for other schools.

■ It is unlikely that equality and fairness is best served by MATs always appointing from within.

**An ethical leader will ask:**

1   Is the school virtuous in its internal dealings? Are staff treated consistently and fairly, not according to whim or temperament?

2   Do working practices make it hard for a teacher to be a good parent to his own children? Is workload consulted upon and set out in published agreement?

3   Is the Trust playing its part as a system leader to increase recruitment and retention?

4   What do exit interviews tell you?

**An ethical leader will:**

1   Develop a plan thoroughly to meet the requirements of the Public Sector Equality Duty.

2   Listen to leavers about their experiences and seek to improve working conditions.

3   Ensure that references are always honest.

## Integrity and behaviour

**Integrity:** leaders must avoid placing themselves under any obligation to people or organisations that might try inappropriately to influence them in their work.

Before acting or taking decisions, they must declare and resolve openly any perceived conflict of interest and relationships.

> Ofsted suggested that reducing exclusions and improving attendance would be the first step along the road to improving results when they visited three years ago. You're a proudly inclusive school and have worked with some very hard-to-reach parents in a difficult Year 9 group. You've agreed that, working together in partnership, badly behaved children who would otherwise be excluded can be counselled by the school specialists and then sent home to work it through with parents for a day, coded as 'educated offsite'. You've a new attendance officer who's told you this is wrong.

A school cannot achieve anything of value without reliably good behaviour. Good behaviour relies upon strong professional relationships between adults and children, highly skilled teaching, robust support services inside and outside school, and intelligent, informed reflection. All behaviour is a language of communication: every child deserves an adult who will seek to interpret the language he is using.

Teaching and learning good behaviour is a skill undervalued in our schools. It is very difficult to do it well. Shortcuts are tempting and sometimes serve as new-minted doctrines to sweep away perceived compromise and failure of the past.

Building a model society cannot be done through inhumane practices. Children's good behaviour should be grown in a context of kindness with supporting structures. Political language used in law enforcement such as 'zero-tolerance' or 'relentlessness' is entirely wrong for children.

One of the purposes of schooling is to model and perpetuate the behaviour needed in a good society, a just and sustainable democracy. Schools are the proving grounds for this behaviour. Young adult citizens are no longer trapped in menial patriarchal industrial structures or domestic servitude. They must be given some space for personal decision-making in school so that when they leave they will be self-moderating.

**Integrity** demands that you do the right thing despite conflicting interests. In this case these are Ofsted, the law and your beliefs.

**Points to consider:**

- Maintaining good order in a happy and safe school community is fundamental to a good school. It takes planning, determination and sheer hard work.

- Achieving it is life-changing for young people from chaotic, neglectful, cruel or violent homes.

- Safeguarding is best served at a universal level by improving attendance.

- Attendance relies on parents knowing that the school fulfils its attendance duties consistently.

■ A school using such 'agreements' fraudulently improves its attendance and reduces its exclusions. The Attendance Officer is right.

**An ethical leader will ask:**

1 Is behaviour management well-enough resourced?

2 Is sorting behaviour and attendance or GCSE outcomes more important?

3 Is there a wider partnership with parents?

4 Do governors know what is happening?

**An ethical leader will:**

1 Formalise all exclusions.

2 Work with staff and governors to overhaul systems and set true targets.

## Accountability and budget

**Accountability:** leaders are accountable to the public for their decisions and actions and must submit themselves to the scrutiny necessary to ensure this.

Times are hard for everyone and the Trust's budget is dangerously stretched. You're asked to provide a forecast beyond this year and you don't expect it will meet the standards set out in the manual. Three years looks grim, five years catastrophic. Everybody knows that budget forecasting is inaccurate in school because funding settlements change so often. If Head Office moves some money from school to school, you can make it through another couple of years before disaster strikes.

It's OK for the Local Authority schools; they can declare a deficit and get the authority's help. As a Trust, it could spell the end of the line. Your schools are doing really well and parents like your approach. How clear do you need to be about the money?

Schools have to budget with probity and according to strict guidelines set out by government. They have to report accurately. It is true that forecasting in the public sector is notoriously hard and three- to five-year forecasts rarely deliver what they promise. However, school budgets are made with public funds and they are public documents.

Schools facing difficulties have to choose what to do. Honesty about the situation may risk your MAT's survival. Resolving it will require lasting cuts that will affect staff and children. Shuffling the money around may just postpone the inevitable.

Schools have finite resources and at the time of writing, shrinking funding. Services previously provided are no longer affordable. School leaders must choose what to fund. School leaders must also be honest and open.

**Accountability** means that leaders are accountable and open to scrutiny. Decisions should be taken openly and transparently.

**Points to consider:**

▨ The financial structure of MATs requires solvency and probity.

▨ Difficult decisions in a MAT may pit one school's needs against another.

▨ Decisions will require judgement about activities previously all seen as essential. Pastoral support and inclusion will need to be balanced against curriculum costs. Is it best to fund a basic curriculum and have flexibility for inclusion needs or a broad curriculum that caters for more students? Should every activity be self-sustaining? If a school is the last in the local area to offer A level music, should that take priority over counselling?

▨ In a universal-provision institution such as a school, it is impossible to disburse funding so that each child's individual needs are met. School leaders need to meet each child's right to the best education consistent with a good education for all children. This has to work well for all children equally.

▨ Difficult decisions, once made, should be explained clearly. '*I chose this path because it is the best we can afford.*'

**An ethical leader will ask:**

1   What are the spending priorities of the MAT? How and where are those decided?

2   What is the quality of the leadership in the insolvent school?

3   Are governors and trustees sufficiently skilled so that open discussion about budgeting decisions may be genuinely challenging and informed?

4   Is prudent budgeting and spending in school informed by openness about, for example, pay structures?

5   What are the top-slice costs of the MAT?

**An ethical leader will:**

1   Always respond to accountability measures truthfully no matter what the risk.

2   Have systems in place which ensure that accountability requirements are fully and openly met.

## Leadership and admissions

**Leadership:** leaders should exhibit all the Principles for Public Life in their own behaviour. They should actively promote and robustly support them and be willing to challenge poor behaviour wherever it occurs. Leaders include both those who are paid to lead schools and those who volunteer to govern them.

> The local area is unbalanced with more boys' than girls' schools, meaning that the mixed schools are girl-heavy. The Local Authority boys' school next to your lead school has been struggling and is undersubscribed, but is now showing green shoots of recovery under a determined new head. Your MAT could do well with a boys' school, though it would make your neighbour's difficulties greater and might endanger their survival. You've put together a proposal.
>
> There's a head down the road whom you respect. He pours you a coffee and clears his throat. He says 'ethical leaders should challenge other leaders whose activities make some children's lives harder'. You're outraged but you like the man.

Schools should serve their communities equitably. However, the easiest way for a school to improve its outcomes is to admit more children who achieve easily: clever children, children from highly aspirational families who place a high premium on education, girls.

A school's success also relies on stable and predictable funding. This is guaranteed by being full, preferably oversubscribed. Manipulating admissions to fill a school with children from supportive backgrounds may leave undersubscribed schools facing the twin challenges of hard-to-reach parents and unpredictable income.

The rhetoric of parental choice and the freedom to set up new schools has a superficial attraction. However, it has brought turbulence into the system. Girls' schools in a particular area will affect the populations and outcomes of mixed schools. Free Schools may endanger already-struggling schools serving the most disadvantaged. Successful MATS are encouraged to expand and share their expertise, but the most challenging schools are unattractive. These may be frequently, expensively and unsuccessfully rebrokered, or left as unsponsored 'orphan schools'.

Schools do not serve society well if one school's success relies on another's failure. That leads to inequalities in the system upon which market-type forces work too slowly. Every child has a right to a good education which will meet her needs. All schools should be good schools, and where necessary, supported intensively until that is reliably achieved.

Leadership is for the whole system, using all of the Principles, not just the ones that suit a particular context or ambition.

**Points to consider:**

- An unattractive child in performance-table terms has as much right to education as an attractive one.

- A school is not a business that may be allowed to wither and fade: it contains children who need to be educated with brio and gusto for every day of their schooling.

- The modelling of virtuous character to children requires schools to support and not undermine one another.

- Unregulated quasi-entrepreneurial activity harms the system. There may be ways in which schools guarantee their own survival at the expense of those serving the most disadvantaged.

**An ethical leader will ask:**

1   What local consultation led to the decision to propose a new boys' school? How was this presented in discussion with the Regional Schools Commissioner?

2   To whom do parents or local colleagues complain if student recruitment activities are unethical?

3   How will the new school serve the most disadvantaged?

4   Such a go-getting leader will be well known locally. What example of leadership is being shown?

**An ethical leader will:**

- Act in a way that builds up the system for the good of all children.

## Trust and community

**Trust:** leaders should be trustworthy and reliable. They hold trust on behalf of children and should be beyond reproach. They are honest about their motivations.

> You're a mainstream school on a brisk journey to excellence. The children are orderly and motivated and you've achieved this by high expectations and consistent implementation. You make sure that potentially difficult students have the opportunity to leave in Year 9 and you make sure that parents understand their right to educate at home, if transfers can't be found. This prevents the children failing and ending up with an exclusion on their record.
>
> Some parents are confused by this so you help them with ready-printed letters to say they'll home educate. Some of them don't have much English so this is helpful to them, a demonstration of your support for the most vulnerable.

Schools serve local communities. Despite the rhetoric of parental choice, most parents happily opt for their local school, certainly where transport is limited, outside of the big cities. Parents often send their children to the same school they went to themselves.

The traditional concept of *in loco parentis* means to parents that they can trust school leaders to do their best for their children. They understand that schools have complaints procedures, communications methods, parents' evenings, coffee mornings, parent and Local Authority governors and such like. They feel confident if they know their child's teachers or head of year. Some like to have direct access to the head and the most determined can usually find a route.

Parents may not be familiar with the implications for community access of contemporary school structures. A MAT will have a Chief Executive who may or may not know their child's school, let alone the child. Some schools don't have parent governors anymore and parents are surprised when they ring County Hall to complain that County Hall has no authority over the school. Parents may wonder who is accountable for the standard of education in the school. To whom can they turn in times of confusion or anger?

**Trust** requires trustworthiness. This pathway is not best for the child and is informed by accountability pressures which the school is not explaining.

**Points to consider:**

- Most parents trust the school to model correct behaviour. They also expect consistent honesty.

- This activity targets vulnerable families who are unfamiliar with the law.

- The complaints procedure may be very complicated, especially if there is no one independent to advise parents.

- The outcomes for permanently excluded students are very poor.

- The outcomes for home-educated students are hard to scrutinise.

**An ethical leader will ask:**

1   What characteristics do the children's issues with these letters share?

2   What is the Trust's complaints procedure?

3   Who represents parents at the school? Is there a local governing board to complain to?

4   How many other students have left to be home educated?

5   Do governors and trustees know this is happening?

**An ethical leader will:**

1   Always work within the law, regulations and guidance about excluding pupils from school.

2   Make sure that vulnerable families – for reasons of behaviour or language – are treated fairly and respectfully.

3   Enable governors or trustees to scrutinise such decisions.

## Wisdom and curriculum

**Wisdom:** leaders should use experience, knowledge, insight, understanding and good sense to make sound judgements. They should demonstrate restraint and self-awareness, act calmly and rationally, exercising moderation and propriety as they serve their schools wisely.

> Your 11–16 school has OK results and sits on a good judgement. You've had a bit of staffing turnover and are trying to work out what the future holds. Its sensible plan is to meet the accountability requirements so you're working towards focusing the curriculum that way. You've made sure that English and maths have a large allocation of curriculum time. Given the state of budgets, the range of other options will be small in KS4, but as you've put all of the arts and practical subjects on carousel in KS3, you've saved money that way and have the teachers you need to cover that and an Art group in KS4. You had more choice when you were at school, but there were too many mistakes made in those days.

Education requires a curriculum to be taught. Providing teachers and specialist accommodation is the biggest cost in a school. The British education system assumes a core of academic disciplines which children should know.

Children have a right to knowledge which is useful, interesting, helps them to prosper in life and aids their development. Therefore, a curriculum should have a core of knowledge valued by society – perhaps summarised as Arnold's 'the best that has been thought and said'. It should have sufficient content to enable a wider worldview and sufficient time for a child to absorb and understand what she has learned. It should be broad and balanced, offering experiences in a wide range of subjects.

Children learn at different speeds and in different ways. The art of the teacher, the pedagogue, is to devise ways of helping every child learn what is necessary as defined above. A child who finds learning difficult will also require highly skilled teachers and reduced content or different courses.

A school leader must therefore use **wisdom** to decide what curriculum to provide, why, to whom, and how to afford it.

**Points to consider:**

- The delivery of a curriculum through its teaching and assessment methods should reinforce the value of learning as an end in itself and persistence as a desirable character trait. A school would not wish to set an example of short-circuiting assessment requirements or underplaying the acquisition of basic skills.

- Accountability measures focus on a selection of traditional subjects. There are others, more complicated to assess, which give greater scope for creativity and self-expression, and which develop a different range of skills.

■ A school's curriculum should offer the same opportunities to all children, whether they are easy to teach or quite the opposite. Schools should resist the temptation to offer the latter a curriculum which restricts their access to future success, participation in civil life and democracy.

■ Schools need to provide support for those who struggle to engage with education for whatever reason.

**An ethical leader will ask:**

1   Is the curriculum sufficiently broad and balanced ?

2   Do alterations serve the needs of all the children in a school?

3   From time to time political, financial or other pressures will make principled curriculum decisions harder. Leaders' first duty is to serve the children, not protect themselves from criticism. What really lies behind this decision?

4   Is there an equality issue? Who will suffer as a result of this decision?

5   Is this a rational and moderate response to an accountability pressure?

**An ethical leader will:**

■ Have a set of underlying curriculum principles reviewed annually by governors against which all decisions are taken.

## Kindness and inclusion

**Kindness**: *leaders should demonstrate respect*, generosity of spirit and good temper. Where unavoidable conflict occurs, difficult messages should be given humanely.

So many disadvantaged children lead chaotic and frightening lives that school is their only respite. It has to be utterly predictable and calm. You've imposed a zero-tolerance behaviour system of unrelenting inflexibility. Silent corridors and family dining make sure that at no moment of the day is a child left to the mercy of himself or his peers. Any child unwilling to live by these rules is asked to leave, permanently excluded if necessary. You serve this very deprived community well and offer those willing to work with you access to a quality education. It is a blueprint for success, scaleable to all schools.

Leaders need to make cool and rational assessments in which the aims of education and the school are met for the largest number of students, most equitably. Behaving openly, they will explain the different and conflicting forces behind a particular decision. They should use the language of informed professional choice and decision (*I have decided that this is the best course of action*) rather than claim instruction by a shadowy superstructure *(I have to do this because Ofsted/the DfE/ the governors say so)*.

Schools include children with all kinds of needs. Sometimes a school may need to exclude a child whose behavioural needs cannot be met, or whose actions threaten the school's communal safety or integrity.

Children are entitled to an education which respects their rights as a child: to free expression and association within reason, for example. If those rights are to be denied, by a school taking an inflexible line, parents and society might wish to see evidence which proves that such an approach is likely to benefit young people's life-chances.

Where a leader decides that a particularly radical approach is necessary for the common good, it should be explained carefully and sensitively.

**Points to consider:**

■ This is the basic utilitarian dilemma of schooling: the needs of the many against the needs of the few. How will this school respond to a needy or traumatised child, whose behaviour requires intensive and personally tailored support?

■ Is the language of the battlefield ('zero-tolerance', 'relentless') suitable for children?

■ The rights of the child are clear; his best interests must be served. But what if that harms the best interests (to an uninterrupted education) of the majority of classmates? While we may believe that education should be funded so that all children's needs can be met in the mainstream, this is not currently so. The *veil of ignorance* requires our social structures to work for everyone equally. How can we do that?

**An ethical leader will ask:**

1   Is this approach legitimate?

2   Does this approach prepare young people for the responsibilities and freedoms of adult citizenship?

3   Will the community support this approach?

4   How does this approach demonstrate my responsibility *in loco parentis*?

5   Where will cases be discussed and experience gathered to see how well this approach is working?

**An ethical leader will:**

1   Work in such a way that builds up the whole education system.

2   Work closely with the Local Authority or Regional Schools Commissioner to provide support for children who cannot thrive in such a context.

# Justice and selection

**Justice:** leaders should be fair and work for the good of all children from all backgrounds. They should seek to enable all young people to lead useful, happy and fulfilling lives.

> You're head of an ancient grammar school with an agreement to open a Free School in a local area where places are badly needed. You'd planned for an all-ability school, but there's a head of steam building about opening a grammar school annexe instead. A team of parents are campaigning very effectively for this and the local MP has let it be known that he thinks it's a sensible thing to do – public demand and all that. It wasn't what you thought you'd do.

Schools exist in history, so some schools have historical attributes which are anachronistic in the modern world. The selection of children by a single test for academic aptitude during Year 6, when they are 10 or 11, is one such anachronism. Evidence shows that intelligence is not fixed at any point and such testing privileges socially advantaged over disadvantaged children.

Schools exist in society and the British search for meaning is particularly troubled. Notions of class and elitism still exert a hold on the popular imagination. Aspirational parents' fear of their clever children being held back by hordes of misbehaving children remains strong in some areas. Arguments are presented partially. Reintroducing selection is bathed in a rosy glow of post-war education policy when a wrecked and broke nation sought to educate a small number of children to build a better world. The promise is of 'clever children plucked out of poverty', not 'most children will go to secondary modern schools'.

Each child has a right to the best education that the nation can give. In a national system, that individual right has to be compatible with the best rights for everybody.

**Justice** requires schooling to be fair, and work for the good of all children.

**Points to consider:**

- Selection models notions of fixed intelligence and the validity of a two-tier class-based education system to children. This does not model virtuous character to children in two ways. First, it is poor research. Second, it justifies a fixed view of fellow citizens' worth based on one test in childhood. The model society it builds up is retrogressive, out of date, limiting.

- Young children are drilled endlessly for selection tests. They unavoidably bear the weight of their parents' hope that they will pass.

- Selection exists within our system, however, and is periodically supported by Conservative governments.

- Poor and disadvantaged children have limited access to selective schools and perform less well when they then go to them. Selection disadvantages most children. It actively harms equality.

**An ethical leader will ask:**

1   Why are these parents' views more important than the original plan?

2   Who will provide education for the unselected majority?

3   Selection was a particular choice in days gone by. Why are we ignoring the current evidence that it is unjust?

**An ethical leader will:**

1   Work in such a way as to quell the fears and beliefs which compel parents to seek selection.

2   Seek to make good non-selective schooling for the model society the dominant provision.

## Service and accountability pressures

**Service:** *leaders should be conscientious and dutiful.* They should demonstrate humility and self-control, supporting the structures and rules which safeguard quality. Actions should protect high-quality education.

---

You're a MAT CEO. Progress is proving hard to pull up in a new group of schools you've taken on and you're thinking about how to motivate people. In September you clearly explained that Appraisal will be linked to reaching aspirational targets and in October you adjusted all targets upwards. You've told the schools that it's not a matter for discussion. You'll set all their targets; they've just got to get them or face the consequences.

Your trust heads' meeting wants to talk about how progress measures and altered inspection priorities make it harder to meet targets which are a long way from students' grasp. You tell them they're apologists for failure.

---

Accountability pressures are exceptionally strong in the British education system. They have been embedded in school leaders through their own education as well as their initial and on-the-job training. As I write, current pressures are upon **progress** – giving greater weight to a restricted group of subjects and **outcomes** which generate the progress measure. These are published as the performance of the school and, necessarily, its headteacher. Therefore, a headteacher must decide whether the school's provision both meets the educational needs of children or the accountability pressures on the school. If not, which takes priority?

Accountability measures should assess the effectiveness, efficiency and probity of the system insofar as it meets the needs of the maximum number of children.

They should measure all the desirable outputs of schooling, whether that is easy or not. Accountability judgements should be the product of educational provision, not their raison d'etre.

In the past, some schools reached high targets by using easier qualifications or teaching children examination tricks at the expense of deep knowledge. That is no longer a route to performance-table success.

A leader will **serve** best by exercising good judgement and analysis for the good of children. They should remember that they serve temporarily and act in such a way that good education may reliably be sustained into the future.

**Points to consider:**

▧ Schools should model honesty in their decision-making and not seek to erect an edifice of educational justification upon pursuit of accountability success.

▧ The UNCRC requires all decisions to be made in the best interests of the child. Therefore, education should primarily serve his needs moderated only by the practical limitations of the school.

▧ Leaders should not devalue the currency of examination results or de-skill professionals by their practice.

▧ Accountability is a legitimate and sensible activity of the state. A good public servant will be conscientious in meeting the standards set by the state.

**An ethical leader will ask:**

1  Is target-setting based on the needs of the child or the aspirations of the school?

2  Do leaders and governors or trustees discuss accountability pressures and share an approach to meeting them?

3  Who offers proportionate and realistic support if a school is struggling with all or some of the measures?

4  Does this approach endanger the integrity of examinations and outcomes?

**An ethical leader will:**

1  Build up target-setting from prior attainment and reasonable targets.

2  Use the professional expertise of teachers to plan to raise attainment.

3  Work in partnership with fellow professionals, listening and responding to their judgement for the good of all children.

## Courage and results

**Courage**: *leaders should work courageously in the best interests of children and young people.* They protect their safety and their right to a broad, effective and creative education. They should hold one another to account courageously.

You're working hard to sort out a school you were glad to take on in your first headship. It's been through some hard times and the teacher shortage means that there isn't the strength in depth yet to guarantee good progress for all the children. Results for the last two years have been well below national expectations, but the governors trust you. The results come out this week and you can't sleep or eat for worrying. You're ashamed of your inability to do better and you're sure everyone's talking about how hopeless you are. Staff like you but how can you face them again with poor progress? Surely the school would be better off without you. Tearfully, you ask the Chair of Governors for a meeting.

Examination and test results mark the boundaries of the head's year. Despite recent rhetoric, it takes time to build up a good school and even the best of schools will have years when results are lower than they might be.

It is impossible to provide quality education for children without a supply of quality teachers. Where heads constantly make do with sub-optimal staff, both education and examination results will suffer.

It has become commonplace to compare headteachers' job security to football managers, where a run of poor results will lead to dismissal. Schools are not football teams, however, and winning children are not transferable for cash. Heads do even worse than the analogy suggests. They often can't get another post, and they don't get payoffs that enable them not to work until their shame dissipates.

Challenging schools which are often in challenging areas benefit from stable, committed, long-term leadership. This gives parents the confidence to trust the school.

**Courage** might mean perseverance against the odds to build up provision from the roots.

**Points to consider:**

- Heads and chairs of governors share the joys and burdens of school leadership if the relationship is good.

- An experienced and wise Chair will have a long-term plan for the school, of which the appointment of a head is a crucial part. The children will be best served by a visionary and conscientious head staying the course.

- It is hard for heads to see themselves as they really are, and stress magnifies difficulties.

- Accountability rhetoric can be brutal. The siren calls of instant solutions are hard to ignore.

- Headteachers burn out quickly.

**An ethical leader will ask:**

1   What were your plans for the year? Did you achieve them?

2   What has gone well this year?

3   What did you say you would do at interview? Have you done it?

4   Who is giving you professional support?

5   What would happen to the school if you resigned? And your family?

6   What kind of help do you need?

**An ethical leader will:**

1   Support a good headteacher to do a job systematically.

2   Exercise care for the personal well-being of a headteacher.

## Optimism and new starts

**Optimism:** *leaders should be positive and encouraging.* Despite difficulties and pressures we are developing excellent education to change the world for the better.

> It's not much to look at. Three collapsing buildings on both sides of a main road, the home of a school that's failed several times before. All year groups have lots of spaces and the staff are a mixed bunch. Behaviour is shocking and the older children are frankly unconvinced by the new uniform. The senior team have all got new job descriptions and you've got your fingers crossed that they can do what you need them to do. It's not going to be easy, but the new Chair of Governors is clever and resourceful and the Director thinks you're just the one for the job. A new building is promised, which is nice. You've not done this before and you wonder if you can, but you've planned things carefully and now you've just got to start. Best foot forward.

Schools are where society looks after its young. New schools and new starts happen all the time and better provision is built on the lessons of the past. Good people take hard jobs and the purposes of the state are fulfilled.

Children start each year afresh and their youth means that can rely on them changing and growing. Our schools give them the chance to be the best they can be.

The new head above wants to do the job well and set a good example for the children. Some of the smaller ones have already mixed her up with the saint that the school's named after. She knows that there's only one question to ask, so she puts on her best smile and asks Year 7:

■ How can this school change the world for the better?

# 15 Leadership in the leadership group

## What do you think of this?

**Leadership Qualities in the Leadership Group**

At Thomas Tallis we expect that all members of our community who have leadership roles should:

1  Show vision, conviction and authority and lead by example.

   Build a team through a clever combination of dynamism, sensitivity, innovation, managing, monitoring, evaluating, praising, supporting and communicating with staff.

2  Understand what needs to be done, do it right, and on time.

3  Be very, very organised.

4  Fulfil your role in whole school leadership by positively upholding our procedures and Plan.

5  Know your subject and keep up-to-date.

6  Lead learning by demonstrating high-quality work with excellent outcomes.

7  Develop colleagues through encouragement, performance management and providing opportunities.

8  Support our young people by maintaining good discipline and helping them meet high targets.

9　Work with others by building good links with KS2, other schools, FE and HE.

10　Trust in others and be trustworthy ourselves.

In the **Leadership Group** we aim to abide by the Principles of Public Life:

- Selflessness – to act for the greater good, not for our own power, status or relationships

- Honesty – to reflect issues as they are and to be honest with each other

- Openness – to explain our actions and respond to criticism, not just demand compliance

- Integrity – to do what is right, and what builds up a solid and reliable education system

- Objectivity – to make decisions on merit, not because they make life easier

- Accountability – to take responsibility for our actions, as public servants

- Leadership – to act according to these six principles and to enable others to do so too

And these practical demands: we should be:

a　Highly visible so we lead and support our colleagues and reassure our young people. We need to be systematic about visibility and holding others to account for it.

b　Collaborative so that decisions are understood and gather general assent. We need to explain and explain again why an action or procedure is needed, and then implement it.

c　Able to see a broad picture and link it to the school plan; resisting panics, fashions and gimmicks.

d　Resist shortcuts or easy answers and remember that human interaction is rightly costly.

e　Able to investigate, research, analyse, plan, implement and evaluate – and enable others to do so.

f　Concerned for the work – life balance of our profession and the future of school leadership by making sustainable choices, not modelling, promoting or expecting a damaging long-hours culture. Wherever possible, we should reduce demands and encourage professional freedom while maintaining success.

Emails: from 1 Jan 2016 do not send any work-related emails before 0700 or after 2100 Monday to Thursday, or between 1800 on Fridays and 0700 on

Mondays. Resist the temptation to put pressure on other LG members to collaborate in subverting this, please. Keep them as drafts if you can't fit them into the <u>67 hours a week</u> above. (None of the above applies during Ofsted.)

g    United, so that all members of the team support one another – but having difficult conversations when necessary.

This set of guidelines has been put together, refined and adjusted by leadership teams in three schools. It is not revolutionary, but serves to offer some ground rules and reassurances to one another. It will carry on altering slightly, as circumstances and the team demand.

(The strictures on emails, for example, were only added in 2015. I found myself one Saturday in a restaurant lavatory answering school emails from a dedicated and super-hardworking deputy and decided that this was not sustainable for any of us.)

The qualities allow us to work effectively and argue constructively when we need to. They also serve as a useful aide-memoire for teachers with any promoted responsibility in the school. They appear on all such job descriptions but are more useful than the job description itself for holding leaders to account. A job description will set out the parameters of the post, appraisal will set specific targets but the qualities cover some of the human characteristics that set good leaders apart from bad ones, effective ones from shouty ones and exemplar leaders from bullies or the detached. All of this, of course, is in the context of contractual requirements such as the terms and conditions of the *School Teachers' Pay and Conditions Document* or its equivalent, and both the letter and the spirit of employment law and its best practice.

The *Principles* and the qualities above are important because they fulfil the second part of our overall responsibility. It is not enough to do the job well, in accordance with the job description and appraisal targets. We must do the job in such a way that we model ethical leadership to the children and young people around us, and therefore the following generation of school leaders.

This is important because the alternatives are pretty grim. School leaders, driven half mad by accountability pressures and the feverish discourse of educational failure, have found themselves making decisions that are unwise and do not demonstrate good service. They may be irrational and immoderate, and they may make it less likely that good people will want to become, or stay as, school leaders.

The following examples of difficult decisions are drawn from cases experienced by professional organisations' member support provision. Let us consider them in the light of the Framework.

## Dynamic leadership?

A school is RI and you're proud the MAT board has sent you to sort it out. In your opinion, the former head was too accommodating with the senior team so the school drifted. You've warned them they'll need to get used to a new way of working, and encourage them to rise to meet the standard of commitment you set.

When you come back after Christmas you're dissatisfied with progress. Everyone's working hard, out and about in school and in meetings until 6pm most days. You use the peace of the evening and the weekend to think strategically, so you need facts from the senior team then. They're still slow answering weekend and night-time emails, so from January you decide that it's easier if everyone stays in school late to do the work and even meets at the weekends when necessary, just for as long as it takes to lift the school into the air again. You even cooked them a working Sunday lunch. They're young-ish and in generally good health: the fact that some seem to have disorganised home lives isn't the school's concern.

A deputy requests a formal meeting a week hence and tells your PA he's bringing a union rep. You're thinking about the week ahead while at a rugby match on Saturday afternoon so you ring him to find out what's wrong but his phone's switched off. You ask yourself – what's his problem?

You may be demonstrating selflessness with your work rate, but you cannot make this a template for all. It is likely that, working such long hours, you will lack objectivity not only about your school but about the potential of the team members. You are accountable not only to the accountability measure, but for your treatment of the people with whom you work.

You are acting unwisely with such demands and your invasion of out-of-work time is immoderate. You exude frenzy, not calm. Your methods are unkind.

Further, you have boxed yourself into a position where it is unlikely that these people will want to work with or for you. You may well wish to move them all on, but it is unlikely that you could replace an entire senior team at once while keeping the service to the children on an even keel. Some or all of them may need to be removed from their posts for reasons of incapacity but an ethical leader will explain this and use the employment processes and practices available. The processes will bring the desired result if you are right in your assessment. Attempting to work them to death so that they resign is not ethical leadership.

## Charismatic leadership?

You took your school to outstanding five years ago. The community is difficult and the children serially disadvantaged. You've moved up to executive head and, with the benefit of a bit of distance, see that the leadership team, while good in its day, has become complacent. The new head of school is a bright young thing so you agree to have some meetings with individuals. Time's short and the children deserve the best so you don't beat around the bush. You don't want the team to stew, so you call them without notice. Useful training for the new head, you lay it on the line in a series of protected conversations leaving colleagues in no doubt that their jobs are at risk if they're not up to the task. No need to formalise it with a record of any kind, just a useful warning shot. At the end, you ask your young colleague: what have you learned?

This is better practice except for the hint that you won't keep records. Protected conversations are protected in that they are *without prejudice to the outcome*, not because they are deniable. Your young colleague will have learned from you if you have done this kindly and delivered the message humanely, in accordance with the virtues. Now you need to set targets and timescales.

That might prevent you doing the following:

## Accountable leadership?

Your results are poor again and you've hit coasting for the second year running. It's hard to attract children, you've a big deficit and the school won't be full again for years at this rate. You need to lose a deputy, and one of them is past her best. If you had time, you'd compile a dossier, but it would be best all round if she decided to go this year. Her contribution to the team is negligible so you don't let her speak in meetings: a kindness, really, as the younger ambitious members usually laugh at her. Though she's often hovering around your PA you've no time to talk so to get the best out of her, you give her a clear list every week of the difficult jobs an experienced person should be able to sort out for you. She can't even turn those round fast enough. You'll need governors to back you in Capability Proceedings and the Chair asks – what process are you using?

The chair may well ask. You cannot deny someone a hearing or reasonable direction for the post. Nor can you turn a deaf ear to bullying in the workplace. This deputy has given long service to the state: if she is no longer capable of doing the job she needs to be dealt with justly and kindly. Put this right before you have to explain it at an Employment Tribunal.

However, even that is better than this.

## Building a quality team?

You know that Appraisal is a bit of a waste of time so you do it quickly. Both your deputies are at the top of the ISR and working well; it doesn't really matter for them, so you get it done quickly in September with a nice letter of thanks. However, as the term unfolds you're pretty impressed by the new head of maths and by November convinced he'd do a better job than DHT2. When you do the new year's Appraisal lesson observation of DHT2 you find much to criticise.

After a long, interesting and very professional conversation with the new maths man in December you can see what's wrong with the current curriculum plan so you tell DHT2 to put a new structure in place for September, ready to staff it in January. She doesn't present it by the deadline, you go to watch her teach again then tell her she's got until next day to resign or face capability procedures on both counts. In an angry discussion she asks you – what are you doing?

She may well ask. It is inconceivable that someone well known to you who was sufficiently competent to have her appraisal nodded through in September is incompetent by January. You have either been happy to accept a poor level of work for a long time or you have been distracted by the prospect of a shiny new playmate who has brought a new dimension (and sharp elbows) to your attention. (If he's that good, invent a new post.) You may feel that DHT2's teaching undermines her other skills: if so, set about improving it.

This is a tricky area. Senior leaders teach less and sometimes lose the classroom skills that may have taken them to high office. Sometimes they never had them. Either way, any teacher in school has to be effective in the classroom. You will need to be open and objective with DHT2 in order to improve her skills in both areas. You can act, but you will need to admit that you have been insufficiently vigilant in the past: governors may decide that capability needs to be taken at a measured pace, or wait until the next appraisal round.

Heads facing all kinds of challenges may be tempted or even compelled into intemperate action.

## Fair play?

Budget pressures are starting to look serious and you need to save about £300k a year. Starting at the top, you decide to capitalise on a retirement and a resignation and reduce the senior team from eight to five, a gross saving of about £200k pa. It makes sense then to attach each one of them to a year group, for which they will be like a mini-headteacher, taking all the decisions and covering curriculum, behaviour, data and so on.

Initially welcomed by staff as a sound way to save money, there's discontent about inconsistencies between cohorts and the team themselves spend a lot of time meeting with each other to learn skills. On reflection, you probably put the wrong leaders in charge of the wrong year groups so at Easter you tell them which year groups they'll change to as soon as the exams are over. You may have to do this again and perhaps all of them won't be able to step up. The remaining deputy has booked a meeting to talk about 'responsibilities in the team'. You plan to demonstrate strong leadership and tell them to shape up or ship out. Why are they questioning your judgement?

Reducing team size is difficult, but you may have made a mistake. The 'mini-headteacher' model takes time to build and may not bring you the strength in depth that a small team needs as much as a big one. However, this book is not a school leadership manual but a discussion of ethical leadership. Be selfless and honest, admit that it hasn't worked and collectively uncover the problems. You may need the wisdom to invite an independent reviewer to look at it from the outside.

In the end, the service you offer to the state and to the children is more important than forcing through a pet project – especially if that objectively hasn't worked and your team are one step away from dysfunction. Wisdom is required.

That's not to say that sometimes a policy or decision won't have to be reversed quickly.

## Courageous action?

Your Trust has struggled with schools it has taken on, some of which are in really difficult areas. The work is punishing and you suppose it not really surprising that the last head of School x wasn't up to it and had to go after just a year. You think, tragically, that her replacement isn't much better and though he's lasted four terms, you and the Trust have decided to cut your losses and look again. In both cases, you have decided that you don't have the trust and confidence in the head to deliver what's needed.

One of the advantages of taking decisive action quickly is that employment procedures don't get in the way and there still remains a chance that the school will pick itself up and prosper while the children whose education has been most disrupted are still at it. Sad, but true.

School x needs more help than you are giving it. It may need a very senior member of the Trust to step in and lead for a while to stabilise it, or it may not be as simple as poor headship. Your recruitment and appointment procedures may be at fault if you've made the same mistake twice. You can work ethically to address this. You are not working ethically if you use employment law and procedures to treat people badly. Your Trust will get a reputation for cynically disposing of heads cheaply who don't fit a template. The children will be served best by your behaving wisely and calmly, not by rushing to repeat a mistake for a third time.

Senior colleagues have a right to expect that you will treat them honestly and in a trustworthy manner, and that advice you given them about their career trajectories is reliable, demonstrating wisdom and good sense.

## Trimming the ship?

The Trust is growing well and quickly. One of the new schools is a behavioural disaster, but you've got a head of year who'd do a good job sorting it out. He probably doesn't have the strategic planning skills for an assistant headteacher (AHT) post really, but he'd be invaluable putting enough stick about in the new place to stabilise behaviour. He takes a bit of persuading, knows it's a risk, has just bought a new house after a second child.

He works hard and after a year of solid restructuring of expectations and many exclusions the school is a happier place. It's time to think about the future and you want a better quality AHT if the children are to be properly served for the next five years. His old job isn't available any more so you make him redundant. The head of school raises an eyebrow when you tell him your plan and asks you: have you acted correctly?

No. You have acted incorrectly. You need to reinstate his old job at the very least, or train him in the skills he needs to be a good assistant head. This is insupportable treatment.

Your team should also expect you to protect them, giving good advice, using correct employment procedures as well as the human support that should be expected as a result of long service together.

## Right judgement?

You are enjoying the benefits of sitting on an outstanding judgement and your team are strong. You expect them to act professionally and get on with the job. A unfounded rumour starts up about an experienced deputy headteacher having made sexualised comments to an ITT student. You tell him to ignore it. It gathers a head of steam on social media so you tell him to put out a denial to quash it. He joins in the furore with an email you wouldn't have written but it should work. It doesn't; your HR manager is out of her depth and you think the deputy headteacher has become a liability now.

You need better HR advice. Advising him to put out a denial was foolish and risky. Your Local Authority or Trust's legal and press advisors would have given you different advice which you should have the wisdom and humility to follow. Be wary of trying to fix difficult problems alone. The inadvisable actions of each of you may be career-ending for one of you.

The golden rule and the categorical imperative require ethical behaviour that is universalisable and scaleable. The following cases underline this.

## Thank you for your service

After years of successful headship you took your school into a larger MAT, seeing that the economies of scale and teacher supply would build upon your achievements for years hence, a real benefit in a turbulent community. You didn't foresee the relationship you'd have with the CEO and the Trust board. Unprecedentedly in your career you're now criticised constantly, set impossible deadlines, and subjected to 'performance management' that seems designed to expose your weaknesses and catch you out. You're working 70 hours a week, sleepless most nights and find yourself making stupid mistakes. You sat in the carpark in tears yesterday morning and your staff, excited by the opportunities the MAT brings them, are tiptoeing around you. You hadn't pictured retiring for another three years but you probably can't carry on.

It is unjust that a system could do this.

The most experienced need support, and the tools to reflect on the task and the journey. They also need the affordances of a stable and just system itself acting in an ethical way: ethics enshrined in a structure, an artifice, a framework.

## Trusting and learning

Your school is successful and stable, a standalone academy with an outstanding judgement in a relatively prosperous part of town. You were elected to the RSC HTB, glad to be of service. Expecting to be able to participate in improving education for all young people in your region, you are surprised by the decisions in which you are taking part. In particular, you're disconcerted by academy chains taking on too many schools too quickly without any time for necessary due diligence. This has led to under-resourced but ambitious CEOs taking on too many schools in challenging circumstances where you know they lack capacity to support senior leaders who'll take on very difficult jobs. There's frankly staggering financial instability at the heart of one of these trusts and a support infrastructure barely adequate for the two schools they started with. As failure gallops down the track towards them, you're ready to learn about brokering and re-brokering processes, but are surprised at the lack of information you get.

You've decided to stand down, but need to debrief with someone. Who do you go to?

The Regional Commissioner, of course. If that's not possible, the School's Commissioner, using whistleblowing procedures if required. Or your MP. You are responsible to the state, as an example to the children and as a professional bound by the Principles and Framework. You are not at liberty to ignore malpractice or reckless risk-taking with the public purse.

## Politics or education?

You're a local head who has watched a local school go from bad to worse, shielded by a charismatic head who persuaded policy-makers that here was a paradigm from which all could learn. He went, the rules changed and the school's fall was meteoric. Now it's a toxic orphan institution. You're outraged to hear that yet another academy chain has been offered a sweetener to take it on in the form of a partial rebuild (though your own need is greater) and nearly £1m in infrastructure costs while your successful school struggles with a huge deficit. You think this is a shocking misuse of public funds.

You're probably right. Again, you must act.

These case studies serve to illustrate real problems. Such problems get worse when good people are deterred from acting because they can't find common language in which to frame their disquiet. It is hard to be the person who says: 'I think this is wrong' if you fear that everyone else agrees that it is right. The shared language of a common Framework is a good act in itself. It may help others to serve better, and with courage and optimism.

It might even help the two public servants below to talk about their motivations.

## The common good

You've been busy setting up a large and successful MAT and it's a while since you've been among leaders outwith your own Trust. When you meet others, you're surprised by the longevity of old-fashioned thinking. In order to be the best Multi-Academy Trust, it is imperative that management and leadership structures are tight and provide good value for money. When the whole structure of public education is under the control of the most successful chains, then the considerable economies and learning of the new system will develop consistently best practice. The only way to ascertain that is by measuring value for money and outcomes. It is not the business of schools to buttress outdated notions of public service, nor a vague idea of working for some abstract 'public good'. How long will it take before this is established?

## The enemies of promise

You're an experienced head of nearly 20 years' standing. You've got another 7–10 years ahead of you but you fear for the future. Leading a school and its community is complex and subtle but high-stakes accountability measures have turned schools into machines and, frankly, you're wary of some of the CEOs and new generation leaders you meet. They pay lip service to partnership, but you think it means 'potential expansion' to them. You sometimes start to talk about the non-measurables of school life, but you feel that you're immediately characterised as someone who'd happily let children underachieve and wallow in poverty in the name of happiness and creativity. That's not what you mean at all. How can you explain yourself better?

# 16 Governors and trustees

Governors are the biggest volunteer group in the UK and work really hard. Its grown increasingly complicated so most schools have a kind of handbook that might include something like this:

In very practical terms, governance works best for the school when we have people who:

come to all the meetings and stay to the end (we know that occasionally this is impossible)

read the paperwork beforehand and ask us when something isn't clear

trust us but question us

see the bigger picture while taking in the detail

support us and get to know us by coming to things*

help us make wider links with parents

understand our time pressures too

act as our advocates in the community, talking us up

understand and support our quirkiness, learning to speak our language.

listen to the leadership on controversial issues

know when to act as a governor and when to act as a parent

*In VERY practical terms it would be wonderful if governors came into school regularly and not just for meetings. Once a term would give a good picture – once a half term would be lovely. You could:

drop in at break or lunchtime and be with a member of the duty team come on a tour on an open Tuesday morning with some students

drop into a parents' evening and see how it goes

offer to meet informally with one of the senior team, to talk an issue over with them

come to the performances, viewings and concerts

arrange to have a cup of something with the head and think out loud

join us for lunch in the dining room

come and cheer on one of our teams

volunteer to help staff a trip or visit

help set up and run a parents' association

help us with publicity

Sometimes there are things where a governor presence might make an event with students seem more important, or where staff would feel valued if a governor came. Importantly, explaining your presence to students would help their understanding of the school's place in the community, and the duties and attributes of a good citizen. It would give them valuable role models in volunteering.

(*Governing Thomas Tallis* 2017)

All the discussion in this book applies to governors and trustees as it does to executive leaders. In order for ethical leadership to be embedded in schools, these voluntary and statutory partners will need to understand their duties and responsibilities.

The Ethical Leadership Commission's Framework for Ethical Educational Leadership encourages school leaders of all kinds to consider the principles underlying their decision-making. It does not, however, offer performance indicators for schools to demonstrate ethical practice. Our education system has many performance indicators and our aim is for leaders to look closely at the two fundamental questions underlying our collective work and think about their application. This will have longer-lasting effects than developing a checklist for schools to complete and forget.

The two fundamental questions are these:

1   How well do we fulfil our roles as trusted educators and public servants?

2   What kind of role models are we to the children in our care?

The Commission's hope was that governors and their school leaders will wish to adopt the Framework, commit themselves to a thorough consideration of the values and the virtues in their schools, and develop and maintain structures to safeguard them. This commitment can be developed by the school, or arrived at through a series of simple exercises such as those below. No tick box, but a series of questions.

(Throughout, *leaders* refers to professional educators and voluntary governors. The term *head* refers to the most senior executive post-holder in the organisation: CEO, principal, headteacher. The word *board* means the accountable body for the school or group.)

## Governing boards

All boards have three core functions as set out in the Department for Education's *Governance Handbook* of January 2017.

▪ Ensuring clarity of vision, ethos and strategic direction.

▪ Holding executive leaders to account for the educational performance of the organisation and its pupils, and the performance management of staff.

▪ Overseeing the financial performance of the organisation and making sure its money is well spent.

That same document requires six 'key features' of 'effective governance':

1   Strategic leadership (vision, ethos, strategy)

2   Accountability (standards and financial performance)

3   People (skills, experience, qualities, capacity)

4   Structures (defined roles and responsibilities)

5   Compliance (statutory and contractual requirements)

6   Evaluation (quality and impact of governance)

As the document discusses strategic leadership in terms of 'culture, values and ethos' there are recommendations about what kind of people should serve on boards. At this point it is not to do with the skills or experience that governors bring, but how they can build up the character of the school or Trust. It notes that governors are *people who have the ability to preserve and develop the character of the organisation.*

Where this has a religious foundation, the attributes of a governor may be assessed by his or her adherence to the faith in question. Where the school or Trust is secular, how might suitability be assessed? Governors' commitment to *funda-mental British values of democracy, the rule of law, individual liberty, and mutual respect and tolerance for those of different faiths and beliefs* is required. Further, governors should want to *encourage students to respect other people with particular regard to the protected characteristics set out in the Equality Act 2010.* They should assess the risks attached to, safeguard and *promote students' welfare.*

# Creating an ethical climate

## Learning and reflection

Leaders have complex and endless tasks to achieve and complete daily, termly, annually, by cohort and for policy-makers and regulators. It is easy to become so single-minded that the first question, 'How well am I doing as a trusted educator and public servant?' is seen entirely in terms of the metrics of accountability. The second question, 'What kind of role models are we?' should be the more important. Success relies on doing the job well, to such an extent that the nation would be better off if all children followed the example set in schools. Getting good outcomes should be a result of doing a good job, not a proxy for it.

So, our ethical weathervane is designed to give busy, devoted and distracted leaders the chance to look at what underpins the decisions we make. We hope that you find it thought-provoking and useful. We hope that it will help make our schools truly places where the next generation of ethical leaders may grow.

There are activities for boards to undertake to help them think about and embed values and virtues in their work. Each of the sessions are designed to be used as a reflective activity before or after a business meeting. Alternatively, they could form part of a longer strategy session or event.

## Activities

### Session 1: Using the language of values and virtues

1  Read the *Framework*. What questions arise when you think about the values and the virtues?

2  On sticky notes see if leaders can give examples of how they demonstrate each of the 14 words. It is best to divide the words up between pairs or threes. Discuss what you have thought about.

3  In groups of four or five think of five key tasks leaders perform during a year. Which of the words best fits those tasks? Discuss what you have thought about.

4    In the whole group, talk about which of the principles and virtues might be the easiest to show evidence of. Which ones provoke you to think '*It's all very well but. . . .*'?

5    Now look at your plan for this year or the next year. Now that you're more familiar with the words, assign a key principle and a key virtue to each key task. What will you hope to do?

## Session 2: Building values and virtues into leadership working practices

1    What principles underpin the way leadership is exercised in this school or Trust? Are they linked to a motto or vision statement? Are they the same every year or do they change according to circumstance or accountability measures?

2    Remind yourselves of the Framework. In smaller groups united by particular tasks (committee members, people with shared responsibilities) think about the ways in which tasks are completed in your organisation. For example, how do recruitment panels demonstrate wisdom? How does budget-setting demonstrate justice? How does an inclusion committee show service?

3    How might the way you work show your commitment to ethical leadership more clearly? Using a current agenda or task, assign values and virtues to the items. How will you protect that value or virtue in the decisions you take and the way you work?

4    In the whole group discuss any changes or challenges that you foresee when you try to demonstrate an ethical standard through a practical piece of work.

## Session 3: Safeguarding values and virtues

1    It is relatively easy for boards to adopt fine words. How would you know if values and virtues are being flouted in your schools?

2    Consider your HR, complaints and whistleblowing procedures. If a junior member of staff uncovered bad practice, what is the path to alerting governors? What risks and pitfalls are in that path? Could a genuine and righteous complaint be stifled before it reached governors? What protection do whistleblowers get?

3    Consider a statement to publicise your commitment to ethical practice to staff. How will you arrive at it? How might you evaluate its effectiveness? How might you deter or deal with malicious or vexatious complaints?

## Session 4: Management styles I

1    What is the 'feel' of your school or Trust? What kind of leadership style best suits your needs and context? What are the alternatives?

2    How does that style fit with the Framework? Try to agree a sentence or two for each value and virtue which explains the kind of leadership you want.

3    When you review leaders' performance, what weight will you give to the Framework?

4    When you recruit leaders, how might you assess them in the light of the explanation of the Framework you have produced?

## Session 5: Management styles 2

1    Practical ethical leadership and management requires working practices which build up the ethos of the school and the values and virtues you have espoused. Your school will have written and unwritten rules for staff about all sorts of things from timekeeping and dress through the way people are managed to the monitoring of teaching standards. *Should* governors be concerned about working practices?

2    What do you know about working practices in your school or schools?

Choose a simple and a complicated working practice or rule from your school or Trust. How was it developed? How is it shared? How do staff feel about it?

## Session 6: A model community 1

1    Returning to the Framework, consider the way in which these values and virtues are modelled to the children and young people. Does your school or Trust have a set of character traits or virtues *for students* that are explicitly valued and modelled?

2    Arrange a focus group with students of all ages. Ask them how well these characteristics or virtues are known, valued and reinforced in school. Ask them if there is anything about their school's behaviour that confuses or worries them. (For younger children you might want to start with something like 'Are children treated fairly here?' And 'Is there anything about school that is unfair?', moving on to 'What kind of person does your school want you to be?')

Be mindful of the ways in which children are chosen for this focus group. It is best if you get a representative group. Be mindful also of the staff put in the room to help you. Is frank-speaking made easier or harder by that choice?

3    Meet with school leaders to discuss your findings. Come back to the next meeting with a report and any proposal for action you think might be helpful. (You might want to combine this with the next two sessions.)

## Session 7: A model community 2

1   Returning to the Framework, consider the way in which these values and virtues work in school. Does your school or Trust have a staff code of conduct that addresses such things, or is it a list of rules?

2   Arrange a focus group with staff at all levels. Ask them how well these characteristics or virtues are known, valued and reinforced in school. Ask them if there is anything about their school's behaviour that annoys or troubles them. Look at the Framework and discuss how well it is lived in school.
Be mindful of the ways in which staff are chosen for this focus group. It is best if you get a representative group. Is frank speaking make easier or harder by that choice?

3   Meet with school leaders to discuss your findings. Come back to the next meeting with a report and any proposal for action you think might be helpful.

## Session 8: A model community 3

1   Returning to the Framework, consider the way in which these values and virtues work in school. Do your parents recognise them as authentically parts of the way the school works, both as an institution and a place of formation of the young?

2   Arrange a focus group with parents. Ask them how well these characteristics or virtues are known, valued and reinforced in school. Ask them if there is anything about the school's behaviour that annoys or troubles them. Look at the Framework and discuss how well it is lived in school.
Be mindful of the way in which such a group comes together. You may need to find another way to canvass the views of hard-to-reach parents.

3   Meet with school leaders to discuss your findings. Come back to the next meeting with a report and any proposal for action you think might be helpful.

## Session 9: An ethical stance

1   Combine all of your findings into a short commitment statement with some clear aims. These should use the language of values and virtues from the Framework. Agree this with the board.

2   Appoint a governor who will monitor this throughout the next year, and report regularly to board meetings. You might want to explain all this on the school website, and ask stakeholders for their opinions.

3   Plan how you will evaluate your success as a school or Trust that is explicitly and implicitly committed to upholding practice and behaviour that sets the best example to our children.

This simple programme requires time and thought from governors and trustees. In making that commitment, they will improve the ethical capital of our schools and the example we set to the young. Schools and trusts therefore make a positive decision to adopt the Framework, developing local steps to remind themselves of the language of ethical leadership and the need to reflect with wisdom as they go through the year and face particular challenges.

The most important aspect of all of these levels of engagement is that professionals look coolly and closely at their role and responsibility in society and their personal motivations. What can we do to make sure that public trust in us is maintained and improved, and that our children understand how to live well?

# 18 Ethics and qualifications

> Forgive me for returning to my grandmother, born in the year the old queen died. Daughter of a shipyard foreman, she was found to be clever and was sent off to be tested by the Headmaster of the grammar school. The only question that stumped her was 'What was the number of the engine which drew the train that brought you here?'. She thought it was unlikely that the man knew the answer himself, so she made one up. Whether she got in by being super-observant or super-canny remained a mystery. She eventually went back to her elementary school and started as a pupil-teacher before going to a new-fangled teacher training college.

Our qualifications start at the point of entry to teaching, and it used to be at that point that the fundamentals of meaning and purpose were most likely to be explored by the budding educator. The theory of, philosophy of, sociology of education may have been touched upon in a good PGCE course, as well as some subject knowledge and classroom theory and practice. All of these are proper and distinguished fields of academic endeavour and it is deeply mysterious how an educated and civilised nation can have decided that teachers needed only the most basic training, similar to the kind of training first offered to my grandmother a hundred years ago.

I first formulated a concern about this in the early years of teaching schools. A very successful neighbouring school was beefing up an application in discussion with the little group of city heads. 'The best thing is', she said, 'I'll be able to train teachers exactly how I want them'. Amidst the sage nods around the room I was silently appalled, hearing the death knell of teaching as a pukka profession. I knew the kind of teachers she wanted, and they were very different from the ones I wanted. Nor did I want to become a teaching school to breed the kind I wanted. I wanted to be left alone to get them from the universities who'd been doing a very good job getting them classroom-ready for years. I wanted them to carry on doing that, and me to carry on appointing the ones I liked best, and no one to make me have teachers that some other head thought would be biddable and expendable.

After that came Teach First, and School Direct and the disgraceful spectacle of a Secretary of State dismissing the university departments of education as 'the blob'. Small wonder that the theory of education is largely missing from our professional formation now: anything that can't be directly linked to increasing achievement is just a waste of time.

In conversation once with a Polish Special Needs teacher, she made it clear what she thought of UK teacher training routes. 'In Poland', she said, rather uncompromisingly, 'we are all properly trained in pedagogy, child development and educational theory. Not like you'.

But who says that theoretical study is irrelevant to increasing achievement? Thoughtful and reflective professionalism allows for stable and supportive schools, where children may develop and learn and well-qualified teachers are treated with respect. These are the fundamentals of achievement. It is impossible to imagine that thoughtful and reflective professionalism developing fully without a personal theory of the purpose of education, of what schools are for and what teachers are doing in them.

So if school leaders have to be model professionals and good role models to the young they need training that enables them to develop and apply this self-understanding from the start of their careers. This has to include a clear ethical framework, an understanding of the Framework and how to use it to help making those decisions that come gift-wrapped in ambiguity. And it will take time to get it right, for the people and the system. If recruitment and reward systems smacking of desperation are based on an acceptance that people might well stop teaching, before they've had the chance to do their ten thousand hours, then we never get the wisdom and case law that we need, in our schools.

**Trainee teachers** should be introduced to the Framework early so that they understand the critically important role they play in national life. It may even help teacher recruitment if the job's hinterland of serious thought and personal commitment is explained. Teaching may appeal more as a serious vocational option than its current image as difficult and unmanageable in the early years and suited only for superheroes at leadership level. Understanding the fundamentals of serious decision-making, they may be better equipped to analyse and understand why schools make the decisions they do. It may help young teachers aspire realistically to senior roles, knowing that instant certainty is less important as a professional characteristic than an ability to tackle difficulty and act correctly. It might encourage them to challenge the shortcuts and poor practice taken by some leaders, and prevent that poor recent practice becoming permanently embedded in the system.

**Aspirant leaders** should understand the usefulness of the Framework in their decision-making training and be given opportunities to apply it to real-life case studies. This might help address the current gender imbalance in secondary school leadership: some say that women are deterred from senior roles because they lack confidence in their own decision-making. If a collateral of the ethical debate and a concomitant of the Framework was to shift debate so that the ability to see many sides to an issue, reflect calmly and act rationally was more highly prized than gung-ho certainty, we would indeed model a better world to our children

Serving leaders should be reminded of the Framework and encouraged to use it in their work. NPQH and NPQEL should include an opportunity for assessors to ascertain that candidates are able to reflect using abstract concepts and make an independent decision based on accepted good practice, rather than learning right answers or waiting to be told what to do by the regulator.

One way in which all of the above would be made easier is by a more widespread use of the language of the Framework. A standalone course in ethical behaviour might not be attractive, however. It might risk the tick-box, KPI approach which has beset our system in recent years. If ethical behaviour is important then the language of ethical thought needs to be normalised in all of our training programmes.

Here follow some examples of the sort of training materials which might be helpful.

# Initial teacher training

## Introduction to ethical leadership

**Basic or introductory training should present the Framework for consideration as above and encourage trainees regularly to identify the practice of or need for values and virtues. One specific training session with follow-up work and written submission could follow during or as a result of teaching practice**

1   Using the values and virtues identified in the Framework, try to identify an area of school life that would call for the exercise of each one. What ethical dilemma is being faced?

2   Discuss this with another person and then the larger group.

3   Either alone, or with another person or in the whole group consider these questions:

   a   Are there any of the virtues you found surprising?

   b   Are there virtues you would add?

   c   Which values and virtues might you find harder to use?

4   What are schools for? What is the school's role in developing virtuous behaviour in society?

5   Reflect on your understanding of your professional role. Is the language of values and virtues helpful?

A longer piece of work should be based in the school placement.

*Either:* How does your school balance the right of the child to a good education and the accountability imperatives of the school? Use the Framework for Ethical Leadership to explore the dilemmas schools face when designing a curriculum.

*Or:* When permanent exclusion has such a lasting impact on a child, how might it be a necessary act for a school? Use the Framework for Ethical Leadership to explore the dilemmas schools face when dealing with the most challenging behaviour.

**One-hour discussion, based on a 1000-word pre-submitted piece demonstrating that the trainee teacher understands that developing a frame of reference for personal and institutional decision-making is necessary to successful teaching.**

## Aspirant leaders (NPQML, NPQSL)

**Basic or introductory training should present the Framework for consideration as above and encourage trainees regularly to identify the practice of or need for values and virtues. One specific training session with follow-up work and written submission could follow during on-the-job reflection.**

Identify a priority for your school or personal area of responsibility. Identify the values and virtues which have helped you frame a plan of action. Reflect on their usefulness as part of the evaluation of your plan. Have you been able to achieve what you wanted? Have any ethical compromises been necessary? Why?

## Senior leaders (NPQH, NPQEL)

Consider the Framework for Ethical Leadership. Reflect on the needs of your school or Trust by using a current or developing strategic plan or other central planning documents. How might ethical behaviour be embedded in all areas of your work?

# 19 | **Who decides?**

Schools have regulation, qualificatory structures and accountability measures. Teaching does not have an independent professional body, for reasons discussed in the early chapters of this book. That has made it harder for school leaders to find a space to consider matters not specifically linked to what has been discussed in the previous chapters.

In the consideration of professionalism earlier in the book, I looked at the role of the headteacher in the local community, working with and for the state and the scope of *in loco parentis*. An adult choosing to embark upon this career will be motivated by a zeal to serve children and their communities and to try to make the world a better place. This drive is underused in our current system, and valued entirely through the annual achievement of changing accountability measures.

Vision and determination, however, take some time to grow and develop into a vital and life-enhancing service. We would capture more of this motivation if we had a formal, lasting space for the development of the abstract values and virtues of professional educators. Pedagogy and assessment, for example, have to be underpinned by a serious understanding of why a person might want to devote a lifetime to teaching quadratic equations or French grammar to children. What might provide that space?

Ironically, government sought to do this during the life of the General Teaching Council (2000–2012). Established by the Teaching and Higher Education Act 1998, the GTC had two aims:

> To contribute to improving standards of teaching and the quality of learning, and to maintain and improve standards of professional conduct among teachers, in the interests of the public.

And three functions:

1 maintaining a register of teachers in England;

2 regulating the teaching profession;

3 providing advice to government and other bodies.

Failure of the GTC was ascribed to the nature of its inception by government, the compulsion of teachers to join it and the scepticism of the teacher unions which felt that it imposed costs and risks on teachers without any obvious benefits to them. Whatever the actual cause, it was a long way from a recognisable profession-led association in the image of the General Medical Council.

The National College for School Leadership – 'Sandhurst for teachers' as Tony Blair described it – opened in 2002, was collapsed into a smaller regulatory body in 2013 which was itself closed in 2018, to be replaced by the Teaching Regulation Agency. In its heyday, the NCSL could have been a proving ground for ethical debate in the profession and a home for ethical leadership training but it did not survive long enough to do so.

So here is the conundrum for the future. Given that the provision, quality and regulation of teachers, and therefore their discipline, registration and deregistration, is rightly a matter for the state, how might it be possible for the right kind of professional body to emerge and survive, let alone develop the capacity for ethical consideration and moderation?

As I write, the Chartered College of Teaching (CCT) is entering its second year. Using the charter granted by Queen Victoria in 1849, the CCT aims to be the recognised professional body for the teaching profession. It is funded by government until 2022 after which it will need to be self-sufficient, relying on membership and 'charitable activity'.

Extensive consultation at inception generated six issues for the College to work on:

- supporting and enhancing teacher professionalism

- offering access to high quality research

- demonstrating credibility and sustainability

- facilitating the sharing of practice

- teacher wellbeing

- representing and amplifying teacher voice

It is developing a Chartered Teacher scheme, research publications and a 'practice hub', 'evidence-informed teaching toolkits', networks and events. With the medical Royal Colleges and the College of Policing it is part of the *Alliance for Useful Evidence*, which 'promotes the use of high-quality evidence to inform decisions on strategy, policy and practice in the UK and beyond' .

The CCT therefore has much potential for important work within the profession. Designed to represent and mobilise teachers, it could also be a good lodging-place for facilitating ethical thinking among teachers. Our concern here, however, is largely with ethical leadership and so the CCT's incorporation of a Leadership Development Advisory Group should provide a home for ethical debate, the first home of its kind.

Why is this important? Crudely, serious professional bodies have ethics committees and ethical debate built into their structures. It is a hallmark of mature self-understanding. That neither teaching nor school leadership has such an independent body may go a long way to explaining why leaders' ethical behaviour has been so easily compromised by regulation. We are buffeted creatures of the regulator and central government. Our qualificatory and post-qualification professional development has been government-led. Our strong independent bodies have been unions, set up to protect the workforce. We do not have a body designed to allow us privacy and space to think about ourselves, our motivations and our role in society. We should.

## The legacy of the Ethical Leadership Commission

The ELC had a deliberately short life, designed to demonstrate broad support for developmental work. It had three hopes for long-term work:

1   The adoption and use of the *Framework for Ethical Leadership* as a way of introducing ethical debate into school leadership.

2   The inclusion of the Framework into training and qualifications at all levels for school leaders and – eventually – for teachers.

3   The foundation of a committee or other body as an ethical reference point for the profession and government. It would :

    a   review particularly challenging issues of school leadership in the light of the Framework and publish discussion and guidance papers;
    b   allow the potential effects of policy change on schools and children to be considered before implementation.

The Framework is simply expressed. As discussed above, it will be offered as a 'mark' to schools and trusts, with a highly accessible training and reflection programme. It will be publicised by the ELC stakeholder organisations who will also adopt its language, thereby successfully inserting a new set of linguistic tropes into the language of school leadership. These twin thrusts should encourage leaders to retrieve some decision-making for themselves and look beyond the pursuit of outcomes to the more reliable pursuit of excellence in all things. The use of the Framework in training has been explored in a previous chapter.

It is the longer-term ethical leadership of the system in which change must be embedded. The lengthy discussion of professional associations and self-regulating bodies above demonstrates the difficulty of this next task. Where might an ethics committee, perhaps a *Committee for Ethical Educational Leadership* (CEEL), live? How might it be accessible to the profession, relevant and useful to their daily lives and constant dilemmas as they seek to serve the nation's children? How will it build up professional capacity through the case law and inquiry process? How might it be serviced and sustained?

It is important that the CEEL should recognisably be part of the education system but independent of government and regulators. It will be best placed as an ethics committee of a professional organisation such as the Chartered College of Teachers. In that context the CEEL will be a useful part of its service, where teachers and leaders could refer issues for consideration. Published findings could spread through the CCT: confident ethical literacy could be a hallmark of the best professionals.

The future is hopeful. This book exists, as does the work of the commission and the commitment of the ELC membership organisations to changing the language of educational leadership. As Michael Fullan (2012) has said:

> The capacity to judge and judge well depends on the ability to make decisions in situations of unavoidable uncertainty when the evidence and the rules aren't clear.
>
> (Fullan 2012: 93)

Leaders get better at judgement, at ethical decision-making, if they have lots of practice examining your own and others' judgements and decision-making. It is the equivalent of the virtuoso's ten thousand hours. In school terms, it takes about eight years, and all the virtues of the Framework.

Whatever structure emerges around the Framework, we have reason to be optimistic. In its own words, despite difficulties and pressures, we are developing excellent education to change the world for the better.

# 20  Finally

It's Monday morning in school, since time immemorial the slot for a quick meeting with the senior team. You go round the table gradually waking up and looking at the priorities galloping towards you. Year 10 exams, governors' budget monitoring group, preparation of reports for Achievement sub-committee, a tricky EHCP Annual Review, UCAS deadline, Year 7 data entry, a reported fight near the shops after school on Friday to be investigated, finding a new maths teacher from September, a return from exclusion, who's going to the drama showcase?, a difficult conversation with a curriculum leader, argument over the need for a Saturday science session, cover for an absent head of year, a training session on trauma, NQT assessment deadlines and the head's report to governors, trying to predict the future. And waiting for Ofsted to pick up the phone.

From there to the gate, and the cheery hallooing of Chapter 2, and, because it's Monday, parents who need to talk to someone in worry or in anger. Thence to Year 11 assembly, advice on revision and stress management, an uplifting message of encouragement, a warning about stupidity on the yard, the reading of lists and the capturing of lates. After that a quick potter around the school and the week is underway. You get back to your office a bit late for the next meeting and before you know it, it's Friday and time for a breather.

Before break on Monday your operational, strategic and ethical leadership capacity has been fully exercised. You've made decisions that affect individuals, families and communities. You've collectively demonstrated optimism with Year 10 in the sports hall and Year 11 in assembly, service with the budget, objectivity with Year 7's data, accountability in the governor papers, integrity in the EHCP review, honesty in the UCAS reports, wisdom in the fight investigation and the difficult conversation, optimism in the search for a maths teacher, openness in the return from exclusion and kindness in volunteering to be at school until late on Friday night. You've shown trust in agreeing to science's demands, selflessness in making a doomed phone call to the head of year, service and courage in making understanding trauma central to behaviour training, integrity and objectivity in the NQT assessments and a combination of the lot in the report to governors. You've shown courage, wisdom and kindness with parents at the gate and explained the justice of fair sanctions to the latecomers. You could do with gathering your thoughts but that'll have to wait: selflessness requires you to give ear to the single-issue tunnel-visioned colleague who's booked himself in. Tea helps. Courage at noon, when the phone might ring.

After he's gone, you think again about Year 11 and wonder if prayer would help. You lay awake worrying last night about August and you wonder what more you could do. Attendance is good, teaching is engaging and reliable except for the vacancies in science and maths filled by a revolving door of supply teachers, staff work hard and you'll probably manage to postpone budget disaster for another year. You've one child in alternative provision and two for whom you provide home tuition. You've managed to talk with 97% of the cohort's parents. You had to make a permanent exclusion in December but you kept faith with the rest of them, including some pretty intractable characters. You've followed the rules for practicals and coursework and your curriculum is solid and broad for everyone. You don't have any tricks up your sleeve. What more can you do?

You talked to a colleague who came to review you last week. She praised your integrity and your honesty, and said kind things about wisdom and service. You recognise the words from an article you read last week about the Ethics Committee, and you heard them and others from the NQTs you did a session with before half term, a welcome change from the old rhetoric of relentlessness and zero-tolerance that jarred so. You do try hard to measure up to the big principles that brought you into teaching. You want to be a good public servant and a role model for young people and there aren't any shortcuts for that.

This job and these children require you to live simultaneously in minutes, days and years. You scan the horizon and you search your soul. Taxpayers can trust you with their money and their children. Let the phone ring: you're ready.

# Bibliography

A la Mémoire des Enfants Déportés (n.d.). http://alamemoireparis.com/overview.html

Aristotle (2000) *Nicomachean Ethics* (ed. Crisp R) Cambridge: Cambridge University Press

Association of School and College Leaders (ASCL) Ethical Leadership Commission (2018) *Report of the Ethical Leadership Commission to the Association of School and College Leaders' Annual Conference 2018*

Barton G (2017) Email to CR

Barton G (2018) ASCL Press Release, June 2018

Bennett T (2017) *Creating a Culture: How School Leaders Can Optimise Behaviour*, DFE-00059–2017

Bichard M (2004) *The Bichard Inquiry Report*. London: TSO

Campbell DT (1979) Assessing the impact of planned social change. *Evaluation and Program Planning*, Volume 2, Issue 1, pp 67–90. www.sciencedirect.com/science/article/pii/014971897990048X?via%3Dihub

Committee on Standards in Public Life (1995) *The 7 Principles of Public Life*. www.gov.uk/government/publications/the-7-principles-of-public-life

Cullen D (1996) *The Public Inquiry into the Shootings at Dunblane Primary School on 13 March 1996*. https://assets.publishing.service.gov.uk/government/uploads/system/uploads/attachment_data/file/276631/3386.pdf

Department for Education (2011) *Framework for the National Curriculum. A Report by the Expert Panel for the National Curriculum Review*, DFE-00135–2011. www.gov.uk/government/publications/framework-for-the-national-curriculum-a-report-by-the-expert-panel-for-the-national-curriculum-review

Department for Education (2012) *Teachers' Standards*, DFE-000666–2011. www.gov.uk/government/publications/teachers-standards

Department for Education (2015a) *National Standards of Excellence for Headteachers*, DFE-00019–2015. www.gov.uk/government/publications/national-standards-of-excellence-for-headteachers

Department for Education (2015b) *The Prevent Duty: For Schools and Childcare Providers*, DFE-00174–2015. www.gov.uk/government/publications/protecting-children-from-radicalisation-the-prevent-duty

Dunford J (2010*) Review of the Office of the Children's Commissioner (England)*. www.gov.uk/government/publications/review-of-the-office-of-the-childrens-commissioner-england

Earley P and Greany T (2017) *School Leadership and Education System Reform*. London: Bloomsbury

*Education Act 2002* www.legislation.gov.uk/ukpga/2002/32/contents

Elton R (1989) *Discipline in Schools: Report of the Committee of Enquiry*. London: HMSO

Fullan M (2015) *The New Meaning of Educational Change*, Fifth Edition. New York: Teachers College Press

Gove M (2011) *National Curriculum Review Launched*. Press release, 20 January. www.gov.uk/government/news/national-curriculum-review-launched

Gove M (23 March 2013) 'I refuse to surrender to the Marxist teachers hell-bent on destroying our schools: Education Secretary berates 'the new enemies of promise' for opposing his plans'. *Daily Mail*

Hirsch ED, Kett JF and Trefil J (1988) *Cultural Literacy: What Every American Needs to Know*. New York: Vintage Books

Hirsch ED (1996) *The Schools We Need and Why We Don't Have Them*. New York: Anchor

Jebb E (16 March 2016). 'Why our founder Eglantyne Jebb is appearing on a stamp'. *Save the Children*. https://blogs.savethechildren.org.uk/2016/03/why-our-founder-eglantyne-jebb-is-appearing-on-a-stamp/

Kant I (1996*) The Metaphysics of Morals*. Cambridge: Cambridge University Press

Kant I (1997) *Groundwork of the Metaphysic of Morals*. Cambridge: Cambridge University Press

National Curriculum website (n.d.). *National Curriculum: Values, Aims and Purposes*. http://curriculum.qca.org.uk – no longer active

Nolan, M (1994) *First Report of the Committee on Standards in Public Life*. London: TSO

Ofsted (2018) *Guidance. Ofsted Inspections: Myths*. www.gov.uk/government/publications/school-inspection-handbook-from-september-2015/ofsted-inspections-mythbusting

Rawls J (1971) *A Theory of Justice*. Cambridge, MA: Belknap Press of Harvard University

Roberts M (2014) 'Curriculum change and control: A headteacher's perspective'. In Young MRD and Lambert D with Roberts C and Roberts M (2014) *Knowledge and the Future School*. London: Bloomsbury, pp 111–138

Spielman A (2017). Speech to Festival of Education, 23 June 2017

Stewart W (4 March 2011) 'Purge of Ofqual and the "useless qualifications" in ministers' sights'. *TES*. www.tes.com/news/purge-ofqual-and-useless-qualifications-ministers-sights

UNCRC (1989) *United Nations Convention on the Rights of the Child*. Geneva: UNCRC

Waters M (2008) *NC34a Memorandum to the Children, Schools and Families Select Committee*, 17 March 2008

Weale S (1 December 2016) 'Sir Michael Wilshaw: Ofsted's "Dirty Harry" bids farewell to a colourful career'. *The Guardian*

Weale S and Adams R (11 July 2018) 'Inquiry condemns school that barred A level pupils'. *The Guardian*

West A and Wolfe D (2018) *Academies, the School System in England and a Vision for the Future*. London School of Economics, Education Research Group report. London: LSE Academic Publishing

Wolf A (2011) *Review of Vocational Education.* www.gov.uk/government/publications/review-of-vocational-education-the-wolf-report

Young MFD (2008) *Bringing Knowledge Back In: From Social Constructivism to Social Realism in the Sociology of Education*. London: Routledge

Young MRD and Lambert D with Roberts C and Roberts M (2014) *Knowledge and the Future School*. London: Bloomsbury

# Index